Spiritual Dimensions of Pastoral Care

Published by The Westminster Press

Edited by Gerald L. Borchert and Andrew D. Lester

Spiritual Dimensions of Pastoral Care:
 Witness to the Ministry of Wayne E. Oates

By Andrew D. Lester

Pastoral Care with Children in Crisis

Coping with Your Anger: A Christian Guide

By Andrew D. and Judith L. Lester

Understanding Aging Parents (Christian Care Books)

Spiritual Dimensions of Pastoral Care
Witness to the Ministry of Wayne E. Oates

Gerald L. Borchert and Andrew D. Lester, editors

The Westminster Press
Philadelphia

Unless otherwise indicated, Scripture quotations are from the Revised Standard Version of the Bible, copyrighted 1946, 1952, © 1971, 1973 by the Division of Christian Education of the National Council of the Churches of Christ in the U.S.A., and are used by permission.

The quotation in Chapter 4 from *The New English Bible* is © The Delegates of the Oxford University Press and The Syndics of the Cambridge University Press 1961, 1970, and is used by permission.

Book design by Gene Harris

First edition

Published by The Westminster Press®
Philadelphia, Pennsylvania

PRINTED IN THE UNITED STATES OF AMERICA

9 8 7 6 5 4 3 2 1

Library of Congress Cataloging in Publication Data

Main entry under title:

Spiritual dimensions of pastoral care.

   1. Pastoral counseling—Addresses, essays, lectures.
2. Oates, Wayne Edward, 1917–   . I. Oates, Wayne
Edward, 1917–   . II. Borchert, Gerald L. III. Lester,
Andrew D.
BV4012.2.S67   1985   253   84-19581
ISBN 0-664-24562-5 (pbk.)

Contents

Introduction

Guiding the spiritual life of individual believers has been a major ministry of the church throughout its history. The spiritual dimensions of pastoral care and counseling have always been emphasized by Wayne E. Oates. One of his most significant contributions, both as a teacher and a writer, has been to focus the ministry of pastoral care on the spiritual enlightenment and development of both the pastor and the parishioner. It is no accident, therefore, that the title and the theme of this volume, which witness to the strategic ministry of Wayne E. Oates, are concerned with the spiritual dimensions of pastoral care.

Each of the writers in this festival volume was selected to contribute to this work because each has a sense of the centrality of the spiritual dimension so necessary in developing an adequate vision for pastoral care and counseling. The rethinking of pastoral care models is a significant task for both generalists and specialists. Accordingly, it is hoped that this work will be of assistance in the reshaping of perspectives and models as we stand at the horizon of a new era in which the ministry of pastoral care and counseling will continue to expand.

This book marks the culmination of an important festival event that brought together hundreds of persons to honor Wayne Oates. A planning committee was appointed by Roy L. Honeycutt, president of the Southern Baptist Theological Seminary, on June 10, 1982, composed of Edward E. Thornton (chairperson),

Gerald L. Borchert, James W. Cox, Walter C. Jackson III, Andrew D. Lester, and G. Wade Rowatt. Many other persons also served on various subcommittees. The festival itself was held April 2–4, 1984, in Louisville, Kentucky, and was designated by the American Association of Pastoral Counselors as an official preconvention event adjunct to the annual meeting. Nineteen special workshops were conducted by former students and friends of Wayne Oates on topics ranging from the biblical themes of pastoral care to specialized aspects of pastoral counseling.

Seven chapters of this volume are written by the plenary speakers at the Wayne E. Oates Festival. Each speaker presented a stimulating address and then specifically revised the work to satisfy our requests in order that this book might conform to certain thematic and space parameters. We felt that, unlike some *Festschriften,* or works honoring a great teacher, Wayne Oates himself should make a major contribution to the volume (see Chapter 4). He has been a pioneer in this field and he has much yet to add to the developing of an adequate spiritual foundation for the pastoral care ministry. The final chapter is an appropriate reflective analysis of his ministry.

To the publishers, The Westminster Press, we wish to express our sincere gratitude.

Finally, a word about the editors. We have served in this capacity on behalf of the entire festival committee. We are both students of Wayne Oates, having encountered him in doctoral studies at different schools—Andrew at Southern and Gerald at Princeton. Moreover, we are each from different disciplines— Gerald from New Testament and Andrew from Pastoral Care and Counseling. But in these differences is represented part of the genius of our teacher.

Wayne Oates began his work in New Testament and became a professor in the new discipline of pastoral care and counseling. Moreover, to all who know him it goes without saying that, although Wayne Oates is a Baptist, his influence has reached far beyond the borders of Baptist life and Baptist institutions. He has taught at a number of significant institutions of higher education. Indeed, he has been a mentor to many and a forceful exponent of the spiritual dimension in the ministry of caring to countless persons in various walks of life. To him this book is gratefully dedicated, and any royalties received therefrom are being set aside at the Southern Baptist Theological Seminary to assist with the future sponsorship of other such special conferences on pastoral care.

GERALD L. BORCHERT
ANDREW D. LESTER

Louisville, Kentucky

1

Finding Center in Pastoral Care

Edward E. Thornton

One of Martin Buber's favorite stories pictures the journey we have taken in pastoral care during the twentieth century and points the way home to our true center of meaning and of power. The story is about Rabbi Eisik, son of Rabbi Yekel in Cracow.

> After many years of great poverty, which had never shaken his faith in God, Rabbi Eisik dreamed someone bade him look for a treasure in Prague under the bridge which leads to the King's palace. When the dream recurred a third time, Rabbi Eisik prepared for the journey and set out for Prague. But the bridge was guarded day and night and he did not dare to start digging. Nevertheless, he went to the bridge every morning and kept walking around it until evening. Finally the captain of the guards, who had been watching him, asked in a kindly way whether he was looking for something or waiting for somebody. Rabbi Eisik told him of the dream which had brought him here from a faraway country. The captain laughed: "And so to please the dream, you, poor fellow, wore out your shoes to come here! As for having faith in dreams, if I had had it, I should have had to get going when a dream once told me to go to Cracow and dig for treasure under the stove in the room of a Jew—Eisik, son of Yekel, that was the name! Eisik, son of Yekel! I can just imagine what it would be like, how I should have to try every house over there, where one half of the Jews are named Eisik, and the other half

Edward E. Thornton is Lawrence and Charlotte Hoover Professor of Pastoral Care, Southern Baptist Theological Seminary, Louisville, Kentucky.

Yekel!" And he laughed again. Rabbi Eisik bowed, traveled home, dug up the treasure from under the stove, and built the House of Prayer which is called "Reb Eisik's Shul."[1]

Similarly, we in pastoral care have had a recurring dream—a dream of finding a treasure that would deliver us from the limits of conventional religion, from hypocrisy and from well-meaning but futile interventions in the lives of others. Our dream has directed us to dig under the bridge that carries the commerce and ideologies of our culture, that is, the bridge named science.

As with Rabbi Eisik, we have found the bridge guarded day and night by the captains of our culture. Faithful to our dream, we have continued to circle the bridge from morning until night, day after day, year after year. Could it be that our dialogue with the captain of the behavioral science guard is now directing us to go back home and dig for the treasure we seek under the stove at the heart of our own tradition? Is it possible that, taking our search for treasure back to our theological home, we will find the center of meaning and of power that will bring us and our pastoral ministries to a new level of maturity?

First, I shall point out some of the values we have circled in pastoral care as we have walked around and around the bridge of behavioral science. Next, I shall rip up the floorboards from under the stove at home and see if a treasure is indeed to be found. Finally, I shall explore with you some possible uses of whatever treasure we may find.

The Search for Center

Finding Center in Pastoral Role Identity as Representatives of God

As World War II came to an end, we pastors plunged into the traffic flowing across the health sciences bridge. We were forced to find our pastoral role identity in these unfamiliar surroundings. The doctors had their stethoscopes, nurses their uniforms and procedures—and pastors . . . ? We claimed our pastoral role identity as representatives of God.

Wayne Oates laid his hands upon many of us and we received a priestly identity: We knew ourselves to be representatives of God not only in the pulpits of the churches but also in the temples of the health sciences, the prison yards of correctional systems, the campuses of academia, and the streets of the ghettos.

External role identity was not enough, however. We were still circling the behavioral science bridge. We had not even begun to dig for the promised treasure. And we were far from home.

Finding Center in the Pastoral Function of Caring

What, then, was more natural than to see the ministry of pastoral care as mission. Ours was the spirituality of loving our neighbor for the neighbor's sake. We were getting involved in human crises. We were moving into alien cultures in Jesus' name.

As we risked involvement in human pain, our attention in pastoral care centered less on role and more on the pastoral function of *caring*. Here, surely, we had found center. Behaviorally, pastoral care is about caring. It is caring for the neighbor without pretense and without expecting personal reward. It is caring in the knowledge of the behavioral sciences and the skills of disciplined professional training. It is caring in the faith that a pastor's care-giving communicates a sense of the God who cares. It is caring enough to know how to give first aid, how to see people through their convalescence, how to predict breakdowns and, thus, how to prevent them.

Prediction and control—these are the hallmarks of modern science. Nowhere were we more intoxicated by the possibilities of prediction and control than in imbibing developmental psychology. Pastoral care, along with religious education, drank deeply at the well of Erik Erikson's "eight stages of man." We swallowed it whole—epigenetic principle, invariant stage progression, and an uncritical fusion of both ego and spiritual development with physical and psychosocial growth.

Caring was the answer. We needed only to shape the systems of family life, church, and community in ways that would foster the natural (epigenetic) unfolding of life from one stage to the next. Once basic trust, autonomy, and initiative outweighed distrust, shame, and guilt, the way was prepared for growth into psychosocial and spiritual maturity, or so we thought.

Then came the 1960s and the challenge of the social actionists for us to prove that pastoral care was not just a psychological regression to pietism. So we stretched the image of caring to include systems pastoral care. Paying attention to family systems was a natural for us.[2] Moving into systems pastoral care of the church, of denominations, and other megasystems was more difficult.[3] As alien as systems theory seemed at first, it has now found its place in the orbit of a pastoral care that finds its center in caring.

Finding Center in Being

Parallel to the developments traced to this point was the emergence of a third center point for pastoral care: a person's own being. Fred Kuether saw a progression in the field that culminated in a concern for being and so included and transformed all previous concerns. Kuether traced pastoral care through a series of preoccupations. The initial struggle of seminarians to make a place for themselves in mental hospitals in the late 1920s prompted concern with the question, "What must I *do?*" During the 1930s the social work model of preparing voluminous case studies stimulated the question, "What must I *know?*" Carl Rogers's nondirective and client-centered ideal shaped pastoral care in the 1940s around the question, "What must I *say?*" The human potential movement of the 1950s in its search for personal authenticity reshaped the central agenda again. This time the question was, "Who must I *be?*"[4]

The emphasis on a person's own being shifted the center slightly. Concern with role and function is centered in a spirituality of loving your neighbor. Concern with your own authenticity roots in permission to love yourself—in the spirituality of self-esteem. At this point in the development of modern pastoral care a spirituality of loving God with a whole heart had not yet become central.

The Clue: Go Home to Dig for Treasure

As it was the captain of the guard who gave Rabbi Eisik the clue to go home to dig for treasure, so it is a group of behavioral scientists who are giving us the clue today to go home and find center under the stove that warms our own tradition. I am referring to the new breed of transpersonal psychologists.

Abraham Maslow was the first to stumble out of humanism

into transpersonalism. In his study of "peak-experiences," Maslow made mystic experience respectable in the psychological world.[5] Exploring the inner world of exceptional people, Maslow asked them to describe "the happiest, most wonderful, most ecstatic moments" of their lives. Many of them reported fleeting moments of full humanness and self-actualization that were not only the happiest but also the healthiest, most mature moments ever experienced. The more Maslow paid attention to these "peak-experiences," the more religious aspects came into focus. The "peakers," as Maslow dubbed his subjects, perceived the universe as a unified whole and had a personal sense of belonging in it.[6] Transcendence of time and space and a sense of living "under the aspect of eternity" prevailed. A feeling of unconditional acceptance reduces tension and anxiety about the presence of evil. Mystery inspires awe, reverence, humility, self-surrender, and worship. Fear is overcome, even the fear of death. The "peaker" feels cleansed and healed. The aftereffects, says Maslow, suggest profound religious conversions that change a person forever after.[7]

Early in his research, Maslow discerned that some of his self-actualized subjects had little or no experience of self-transcendence. But for the "peakers," transpersonal experiences formed the central core of their character. The "peakers," Maslow found, more easily transcend their own ego; they are more innovative and creative; and they often awaken transcendent capacities in others. Their vision of transcendent reality leaves them at times feeling a "cosmic-sadness over the cruelty, blindness, self-defeat, and just plain stupidity of humankind." Their transcendence also produces objective compassion prompting them to strike out at evil in constructive and redemptive ways. In a word, the "peakers" project the charisma of a saint or sage.[8]

At this point Maslow's findings challenge the prevailing assumption of behavioral science about human development. Nearly every study of human development, prior to the advent of the transpersonal psychologists in the late 1960s, assumes that the final stage of healthy growth is the emergence of a mature, well-differentiated ego. Maslow's self-actualized person proved to be of two types—"peakers" and "non-peakers." The "non-peakers" fit the prevailing model of full ego differentiation. But the "peakers" force us to face up to the possibility of an entire developmental stage that moves beyond ego maturity, beyond social adjustment, into a transpersonal realm, characterized by higher consciousness.[9]

We now know that the higher consciousness discovered in Maslow's "peakers" is neither a rare and transient state nor a seesaw alternation between peaks and valleys. It is, rather, a stable state of consciousness marked by particular features.[10]

The transpersonal stage of human development is like a priceless Oriental rug that was stolen by a thief. On market day he hawked it for one hundred pieces of gold. A dealer in fine rugs recognized its value, bought it at once, and then asked the thief why he sold a priceless rug for only a hundred pieces of gold. The thief replied, "Is there any number higher than one hundred?"

Contemporary behavioral science still treats the transpersonal stage of life as if it were just like any other item in the intellectual shopping centers of the world. Like the thief, a person who has not experienced the transpersonal stage of development is willing to get rid of it at the going rate for psychological insight, unaware of numbers higher than one hundred. Could it be, however, that a stable state of consciousness that lies beyond ego maturity in the realm of religious experience is the priceless treasure we are seeking for pastoral ministries?

Just as the dream of the captain of the guards gave Rabbi Eisik the clue to go home and dig under his own stove for a priceless treasure, so the research of transpersonal psychologists clues us to return home, to rip up the floorboards and claim the treasure we find there. As we do so, what we find is both frightening and transforming.

Finding Center: The Treasure Is Sainthood

At the heart of the Judeo-Christian tradition, something lies hidden in layers of yellowed wrapping. Carefully, yet excitedly, we fold the wrappings back and claim the treasure: *a childlike awareness of spiritual reality.* We lift it up and turn it slowly— skeptical but transfixed. Every facet is radiant with refracted light. Each facet has a different name.

The treasure is known as illumination and as spiritual awakening, as a higher consciousness and as God-consciousness, as "the farther reaches of human nature"[11] and as being "transformed by the renewal of your mind" (Rom. 12:2). The treasure is not inert. It is alive and growing. When full grown, it is known as the transpersonal stage of human development and as that stage on the spiritual journey which in Scripture is called sainthood.

What could be less to the liking of theologically sophisticated pastors and clinically competent counselors than "childlike awareness of spiritual reality"? What could be more of a scandal than to advocate sainthood as the center point for a socially active, ethically committed church? To say the word "sainthood" feels like bad taste even though it is a basic biblical term.

For most of us, sainthood suggests escapism—like copping out from the real world or being blissed out in states of ecstasy. We in pastoral care are the practical, down-to-earth types. We want specific solutions to the problems of everyday living. Oh, yes, we have had a few peak experiences—probably in our adolescent years. We may even have moments now when we sense a higher power beyond ourselves and a more than normal sense of love, joy, peace, and well-being. But we are realists. We are radically honest with ourselves. We do not indulge in wishful thinking or pious platitudes. We face up to the ugliness, cruelty, pain, and loss in life. We gave up long ago reaching for spiritual perfection or hoping for anything as far out as mystic oneness with God.

Yet, for all of our resistance to the idea of sainthood, the possibility of a childlike awareness of spiritual reality draws us back to the treasure we find at the heart of our religious tradition. We must take a second look.

A study of sainthood is a study in surprises. For instance, saints are rare among religious people. An ancient story makes the point.

Once upon a time a very religious man was walking beside a wide river. He was meditating on the law of the Lord, for he believed that if he kept his mind fixed on spiritual thoughts all the time, he would achieve perfection.

Just then his thoughts were broken by the sound of a chant used in his religion to prepare for experiencing the Presence of God. He was angered by what he heard, for the chant was being done wrong. At each transition where you were supposed to say "ah-men," the person chanting was saying "a-men."

He knew it was his religious duty to go to the person, probably a hermit living alone on the island in the middle of the river, and instruct him in the correct way to do the chant. You see how very religious and self-sacrificing he was, for he put his religious duty to care for an ignorant hermit ahead of his own quest for perfection.

So, renting a boat, he rowed across the river to the island and found the hermit moving in rhythm to his chant.

"Friend," he said, breaking the hermit's concentration, "you are doing the chant wrong. I have come to instruct you in the right way."

"Thank you," said the hermit, genuinely grateful for the help he was being offered.

After instructing the hermit, he went away congratulating himself on his good deed. As he rowed back across the river, he recalled the ancient saying, "One who achieves perfection will walk upon the water without fear," and he dreamed of the day he would be able to walk on the water himself.

His meditation was interrupted, however, by the sounds of the hermit's chant once again. At the first transition there came a faltering "ah-men," but as the chant progressed, the hermit lapsed back into his old habits, saying "a-men" over and over again. You can imagine how disgusted he was with the hermit. His thoughts about the ignorance of human beings and their persistence in error were interrupted suddenly by a strange sight. The hermit was coming toward him—walking on the water.

"I am sorry to bother you again," said the hermit as he approached the boat, "but I have forgotten the right way to say the chant. Would you be so good as to instruct me once more?"

Sainthood, then, has nothing to do with esoteric religious knowledge or with strictly keeping religious rules. Transformation into the stage of sainthood is hard for the learned. A religious reputation is a big handicap. The door to sainthood has no knob on your side. It opens from the far side to those who are unselfconsciously immersed in longing love for God.

Sainthood is something that happens to you in the fullness of time. It is not something you make happen by yourself. As it happens, you see that you have helped it happen. You have been willing but have not willed it to happen.[12] Your willingness is a readiness to be at peace with God, to allow God to be your friend rather than to persist in seeing God as enemy. It is accepting that you are accepted and loved by God. Once you are awakened to the reality that God is love, an inner flame is lit—a burning desire to love the Lord your God with all your heart, soul, strength, and mind, and your neighbor as yourself (Luke 10:27).

Being willing to let God be who he is, i.e., unconditional love, that is the rub. Thomas Merton calls this the problem of "Promethean theology." Like Prometheus of Greek mythology, you may assume a basic, jealous hostility between humankind and God. You try to steal something from God that God does not want you to have. You fear that God does not want you to be fully actualized, that divine grace is opposed to your true self. You are afraid to believe that grace is opposed only to your inflated ego and your tyrannical superego but never to your inmost self. You grasp at self-actualization as a thief, and cling to it, as Kierkegaard said, by willing despairingly to be a self. In this way you shut God out and justify your complaints about the absence of God.[13]

The absence of God fulfills a necessary function on the spiritual journey. It is the spiritual reality on the shadow side of growth toward authentic ego identity.[14] After baptism comes the wilderness. Yet where in the typical theological curriculum do you learn to appreciate the absence of God in your wilderness wanderings? Travel from the land of bondage to the promised land and you must go through the wilderness. Traveling the wilderness evokes the "cry of absence," soulfully uttered in Martin Marty's latest work.[15] At best, you enjoy only an occasional peak experience by which to map the journey.[16] Is it any wonder, then, that pastors and all others who venture into the wilderness in search of self-actualization become skeptical about the mystic reality of the Presence? When you travel for years with only wisps of cloud for direction by day and fireflies for light by night, you lose faith in the possibility of a radiant pillar of light that reveals your "inmost self" (Rom. 7:22) and awakens a longing love that becomes a new and stable state of consciousness.[17]

Against the backdrop of the absence of God, you can begin to see the importance of pastors being awake to the possibility of sainthood for everyone. Sainthood is a pilgrim's compass. You may wander in the wilderness for decades, but if your compass is true, you will never be totally disoriented. Childlike awareness of spiritual reality may happen at age three, thirteen, twenty-three, ninety-three, or at any age in between.

Peak experiences rise out of the plains and deserts of life more often than we know. Most people, including many pastors, discount such experiences when they happen. Many keep them private, feeling embarrassed to share them even with their pastor or in church groups, surprising as that may be. Others befriend their spiritual experiences but do not know what to make of them or how to cultivate the promise they hold for growth into the stable state of consciousness we know as sainthood. A pastor who understands that healthy human growth proceeds from egocentricity to ego maturity and then from ego maturity to ego transcendence responds to spiritual awareness in parishioners very differently from a pastor who sees ego transcendence as a necessary symptom of infantile regression or cultic deviance. Let pastors learn experientially something about the classical spiritual disciplines and the ancient tradition of spiritual guidance, then pastoral care will become a ministry that enhances spiritual awareness at every age and stage and in every circumstance of life.

Sainthood as a stable state of God-consciousness gives substance to Browning's line, "The best is yet to be." Sainthood as a compass for the spiritual journey enables pilgrims created in the *image* of God to progress into God's *likeness*. The *image* of God refers to structures given in creation enabling everyone to be awake to both physical and nonphysical reality. The *likeness* of God refers to growth toward a stable state of transpersonal consciousness. Transpersonal consciousness is being awake to the linkage between your true self and the One in whom "all things hold together" (Col. 1:17).

Rediscover the transcendence of God as the Presence within and your wilderness work is done. God as Spirit illumines your "inmost self." You love God for God's sake. You love your own true self for God's sake. You become amphibious—capable of moving at ease in two realms. You move in the realm of ordinary ego consciousness and in the "inmost" realm of God-consciousness. You discover that God-consciousness and consciousness of your true self are one realm—the realm of "the Lord who is the Spirit" (2 Cor. 3:18). It is a realm as different from ego maturity as ego maturity is from egocentricity. You are being transformed into a growth stage that lies beyond ego differentiation. In due time, you enter the transpersonal stage, which is, in the language of the church, the stage of sainthood.

The Center in Pastoral Care

When God-consciousness and the consciousness of your true self are at one, you find center for pastoral care as well. Pastoral identity does not take root in role or pastoral office alone, or even in the pastoral function of caring. Rather, it is rooted in the human capacity for God-consciousness. The ground of pastoral identity is the ground of human identity and of Christian experience: the ground of being created in the image of God, and of being transformed from one degree of glory to another into the likeness of "the Lord who is the Spirit" (2 Cor. 3:18).

Your legacy in the psychology of religion serves you ill if it constricts your attention to conversion as a single moment of God-consciousness, or if it relegates mystic consciousness to holy people, and sainthood to museums housing the treasures of yesteryear. Your map of the spiritual journey will lead you down dead-end roads if it describes only the passage through psychosocial stages of human growth and development. The repertoire of the ages for attending to the life of the spirit has been veiled too long in the monastic traditions of Christianity, the methods of Eastern religions, and the primitive rites of the shamans. These treasures belong to pastoral care and counseling as well.

Pastoral care has not ignored the spiritual dimensions of ministry altogether. It has, however, become lopsided, restricting awareness to the spirituality of service and avoiding thereby the spirituality of interior prayer. Commitment to the love of neighbor has been genuine but partial. A spirituality of service alone leaves a person flat, two-dimensional, and landlocked rather than amphibious in the realms of consciousness. In such a state, a person is likely to rely too much on professional knowledge and skill and to be blind to the mystery that stirs up a longing love for God.

The spirituality of sainthood both creates and flows out of a wholehearted love of God. Your center shifts from service to worship. Worship is not just a means to further service but is an end in itself. Caring for neighbor becomes not your goal but a by-product of your commitment to hallowing the name of God, that is, to caring for the glory of God, not of yourself. Representing God in the pastoral office happens unselfconsciously. Being authentically present to others is balanced by being authentically absent to them while present to God. In God's presence you become more fully open to the neighbor than ever before, and you become open to the option of intercession as well as of professional intervention. You hang the "In Conference" sign on your office door to protect your time for prayer as well as for parishioners and clients. Paradoxically, you serve your neighbor better. With the treasure found at the heart of the pastoral care tradition, then, you begin to build a house of prayer and of care.

The value of a treasure is measured by what you do with it and what it is able to do for others. Rabbi Eisik dug up the treasure from under the stove in his own house and he "built the House of Prayer which is called 'Reb Eisik's Shul.'" Rabbi Eisik's find was a treasure because he used it to raise the God-consciousness of his people. He was empowered by his treasure to prepare the way for the spiritual transformation of an entire congregation. So what could it mean for you to discover a quality of prayer that generates spiritual maturity? What are the possible consequences of digging at the heart of your tradition for the shaping of an agenda for tomorrow? Here are seven changes you may expect:

1. You may awaken with a desire that carries you beyond ego maturity into the relatively egoless, transpersonal stage of sainthood. You are seeing transformations of this kind in Wayne Oates's recent book, *Nurturing Silence in a Noisy Heart,* [18] and in many others that point the way to meditation and interior prayer. [19]

2. You may invest more and more of your pastoral ministry in the work of spiritual guidance. Leading the way among Protestants to a recovery of the church's ancient ministry of spiritual direction is the Shalem Institute for Spiritual Formation, in Washington, D.C. [20]

3. Seminary professors, supervisors of clinical pastoral education, and directors of training for pastoral counseling centers may become intentional about the spiritual formation of seminarians and ministers in their programs. Retreats and one-to-one spiritual guidance sessions may well show up alongside interpersonal relations groups and clinical supervision of ministry functions. Increasingly, seminars may include classics of spirituality as

well as the classics of personality theory.

4. Undergirding the ministry of spiritual guidance in the parish and in professional training programs is the need for solid research. Pastoral care specialists are beginning already to do pastoral assessment of spiritual growth.

James Fowler has opened the door to research the stages of faith development in cross-cultural perspectives. Spiritual formation within each faith stage needs more study, as do fixation and regression on the spiritual journey. Fowler's hypothesis about the differences and the interconnections between conversional and structural changes in faithing (or meaning-making) also needs to be tested.[21]

Ana-Maria Rizzuto's bold hypothesis about the formation and impact of private god images on her subjects' subsequent life stories requires research among persons who are not psychiatrically hospitalized.[22] Is the transformation into sainthood possible prior to full ego maturation among normals?[23]

Scott Peck's call for the inclusion of the category of evil in the DSM III[24] throws down the gauntlet before both pastoral and psychiatric researchers to examine the phenomena of evil without wearing humanistic philosophical blinders. Peck's courage in reporting cases of possession and exorcism introduces a cosmic dimension into the pastoral care agenda for tomorrow, whether or not it is wanted.[25]

5. A transpersonal agenda may stimulate joint studies by the sociology of religion and the psychology of religion. Ken Wilber has done the conceptual mapping necessary to assess the legitimacy and the authenticity of organized religions in comparison one with the other. According to Wilber, a "more legitimate religion will integrate meanings" within a particular stage on the spiritual journey more fully than a less legitimate religion (comparing adherents in the same faith stage). A "more authentic" religion has the most power to enable adherents to be transformed from one level of consciousness to a higher level.[26] Wilber's assumptions need critical scrutiny, but his challenge to world religions to subject themselves to comparative studies of their power to produce ego integration at lower levels and sainthood at higher levels cannot be avoided for long. Wilber's scheme poses an empirical test of the "fruits" of a worldview or faith system that goes to the core of religious experience itself—

something not yet seen in religious research on an interfaith scale.

6. New horizons appear for understanding and providing pastoral care to persons at each developmental stage and in the crises of life as well. If the normal developmental process rides on transpersonal currents flowing toward the transpersonal stage of sainthood, then the ministry of pastoral care needs to be reexamined at each transition to discern the forms and dynamics that God-consciousness takes in relation to the physical, cognitive, psychosocial, and moral aspects of development at that particular stage.

The dynamics of transpersonal longings in human crises need to be studied as well. For example, religious factors in alcoholism have been well researched,[27] while other behaviors similarly motivated and reinforced by transient mystic experiences are being treated without reference to transpersonal phenomena. Sexual acting out is an example. Ecstatic experience is a feature of sexual orgasm, and for many persons the orgastic ecstasy is heightened by having sex in the context of a forbidden relationship. However, attention to the search for self-transcendence and mystic consciousness is altogether absent from the pastoral care literature on sexual problems. Suicide presents similar questions. For many suicidal persons, the attempt is accompanied by fantasies of death and rebirth. Rebirth carries the promise of perfect unity, harmony, and peace, offering what has not been achieved in this world: that is, a transpersonal state of consciousness. Could suicide be in part a desperate bid for a stable state of mystic consciousness? Could the care of suicidal people be informed by transpersonal research?

7. Finally, new horizons appear for biblical, historical, and theological studies. Transpersonal psychology illumines phenomena such as the revelatory and predictive function of dreams, high vision states (such as Moses at the burning bush or the annunciation to Mary), inspired writing and utterance, the experience of cosmic entities whether angelic or demonic, clairvoyant knowing, psychic healing, psychokinetic phenomena (such as walking on water and withering a fig tree), dematerialization (such as Philip's departure from the Ethiopian eunuch), and even snake handling (as in Paul's experience recorded in Acts 28:3).

Transfiguration and resurrection take on new dimensions of historicity and of meaning in the light of transpersonal research. Pentecost and glossolalia disclose universal human potential at one level and a breakthrough of cosmic consciousness at another. The high visions in Daniel, Ezekiel, and Revelation carry archetypal power and so deserve attention not only as historical documents but also as inspired utterances applicable to every era of history. The theology of sanctification or spiritual journey needs radical reworking today and cannot be done adequately apart from transpersonal and contemplative psychologies.

Conclusion

Once Rabbi Eisik found and invested the treasure his name became synonymous with a place of worship—"Reb Eisik's Shul." Could we hope for more in pastoral care than for the day that our ministries would be synonymous with glorifying God . . . our practitioners distinguished by their own spiritual journeys into the transpersonal stage of sainthood . . . their published articles probing the ministries of guiding others into higher states of consciousness as well as of caring and counseling on the road to ego maturity . . . their research, in cooperation with the whole theological enterprise, raising God-consciousness, making spirituality speakable, and recovering treasures of spiritual transformation long buried and forgotten by a rationalistic theology?

A few years ago I dreamed a dream. In the dream I was told, "The formula $2 \pi R$ will solve everything." Waking, I tried to forget the dream, but the words kept echoing: "The formula will solve everything." So I sat down to center on the dream, to receive its word of wisdom. Soon the rest of the formula popped into focus: $2 \pi R = C$. Immediately I realized that the formula contains everything needed to compute a circumference except the radius. The radius is the shortest distance from any point on the circumference to the center. For me, the circumference of a circle symbolizes wholeness—wholehearted commitment to spiritual growth, wholehearted love for God and neighbor. So then the dream message came clear: Find center and the formula will solve everything else. Find center and you know the radius. Know the radius and you know the shortest distance from where you are to the center. So, *find center and you have solved the problem of finding wholehearted love and care.*

Since the day I dreamed that dream I have paid attention to finding center more than to solving anything else. The dream is true. Find center and the formula solves everything. My hope in offering this chapter is that we may find center in pastoral care. When we find center, our future is assured.

2

Recovering
the Pastor's Role
as Spiritual Guide

E. Glenn Hinson

The title of this chapter suggests that pastors have functioned in the past as spiritual guides and that this role has suffered erosion or at least undergone some sort of radical change. Although each of these assumptions is correct to some degree, I would begin with a warning against undue optimism that every pastor will or even can become a spiritual guide. Whether each will or can, of course, will depend in great part on our expectations. If pastors expect to become Anthonys, Ambroses, Augustines, Benedicts, Gregorys, Bernards of Clairvaux, Julians of Norwich, Catherines of Siena, Ignatiuses of Loyola, Teresas of Avila, Friedrichs von Hügel, or Thomas Mertons, they will overshoot the goal. Of these much-sought-after spiritual guides, please note that only Ambrose, Augustine, and Gregory served as pastors. The others spent their time mostly in solitude and prayer, a luxury most pastors could scarce afford, and these three did their best to do the same.

Becoming a spiritual guide, I think you will find, will involve not the learning of a technique, such as you would do for personal counseling, but paying the price of letting God work you over, being purified by the fire of divine love, undergoing trans-

E. Glenn Hinson was Professor of Religion, Wake Forest University, Winston-Salem, North Carolina. Since delivering this address he has been called as David T. Porter Professor of Church History, Southern Baptist Theological Seminary, Louisville, Kentucky.

formation from within by divine grace. And our work- and works-oriented, success-driven society and churches will not only withhold encouragement for that but will do everything possible to thwart it.

What Is Spiritual Guidance?

The phrase "spiritual guide" is a happy choice which we need to clarify before we try to trace the history of the pastor's role in it. For Protestants it is preferable to the more commonly used "spiritual director," because the latter bears an authoritarian nuance that grates on the Protestant perception of salvation by grace through faith. It is seldom true today, of course, but in past centuries spiritual directors in monasteries often laid heavy hands on those they directed, without consideration for individuality and personhood. By the end of the Middle Ages the practice of private oral confession had become so corrupted, and was so often abused, as to result in its total rejection by the Reformers. You may remember those lines from Chaucer about the Friar as "a wantown and a merye, a limitour" who was "ful wel biloved and famuliar," for "he had power of confessioun," which he heard "ful swetely." We might well ask whether the Reformers did not overreact when they tossed out this important means of spiritual guidance, but, for the moment, we have to keep their objection in mind while defining it.

What, then, will we be as "spiritual guides"? To be a spiritual guide is to be a "midwife" and "mother" of grace. Or, if you are conditioned to thinking only in masculine imagery, it is to be an "obstetrician" and "physician" of the soul. In either case, there are weighty considerations behind the choice of images.

In the first place, these images suggest that divine grace and not human guidance is the main factor in spiritual development. We may plant or water, to borrow an analogy from Paul, but God causes growth (1 Cor. 3:6). It is crucial here, however, that we understand grace in the right way, for from Luther on, Protestants have espoused a one-sided and restricted interpretation which would virtually preclude any effort at spiritual guidance. Protestants have defined grace in forensic imagery as God's unmerited favor in acquittal or forgiveness of the sinner. At the same time, they have denied the Catholic understanding of grace as the Spirit working in the life of the believer to change and transform. Our era of improved relationships and feelings between Protestants and Catholics has made it possible, I think, to see that the New Testament writings, even Paul's, on whom Protestants have focused, allow both views. Grace means God's undeserved gentleness toward the sinner, but it also means God's transforming presence and power to change the sinner's life.

The traditional Protestant definition scarcely requires documentation, but you may want to know from what Pauline texts I would support the Catholic perception. The most obvious is the answer Paul received to his entreaty for removal of his "thorn in the flesh": "My grace is sufficient for you, for my power is made perfect in weakness" (2 Cor. 12:9). Here divine grace and divine power are synonymous. Christ himself, his presence, is enough. Supportive also of this view of grace are Paul's comments about his equipment for ministry in 2 Corinthians 3 and 4 in response to critics. "Such is the confidence that we have through Christ toward God. Not that we are sufficient of ourselves to claim anything as coming from us; our sufficiency is from God, who has qualified us to be ministers of a new covenant" (2 Cor. 3:4–6). "We have this treasure in earthen vessels, to show that the transcendent power belongs to God and not to us" (4:7).

It is grace, then, God personally present, which has to effect change and to cause growth in our lives. We can do nothing to effect "purity of heart," that downright goodness from which flow selfless and loving deeds. The goal of all of us, surely, is set forth in Matthew 25:31–46, a passage whose major focus is on the character of those who know kingdom righteousness rather than on judgment, as it has been applied so often. The "righteous" are those who fed the hungry, gave drink to the thirsty, showed hospitality to strangers, clothed the naked, visited the sick and the imprisoned without even reflecting on what they were doing. They were "good trees" bearing "good fruit." They could not help doing good.

The role of the minister, therefore, is that of "midwife" or "mother" or "obstetrician" or "physician" and not that of a source. We can assist persons as they give birth and we can encourage them as they grow, but we do not account for conception or growth. Sometimes we will help most if we get out of the way and let grace work. At other times we can help someone pry a door open so as to let God's wisdom and love and power flow in. But we must never try to usurp the Holy Spirit's place and function, as medieval inquisitors erroneously tried to do.

Spiritual Guidance in Historical Perspective

Conceived in a broad sense, spiritual guidance should be the overarching integrative factor in pastoral ministry. In Christian history, however, it has usually constituted only one of many roles a pastor plays, even though there is a sense in which everything a pastor does touches on spirituality, or at least *should* do so. Indeed, not only the individual but even the corporate roles of a pastor will have some bearing on the spiritual development of members, whether for good or for ill. Corporate worship, for instance, has a distinct and vital effect on the spirituality of most members and may be the only means through which spiritual guidance occurs. This thesis would imply that the spirituality of ministers themselves is of critical importance, since spiritual guidance may have to seep into the lives of members in indirect rather than direct ways.

Lest my presentation be no more than a shotgun blast, however, I had better confine my historical summary to the more personal guidance given by pastors. This statement will be connected closely with what has been called "the cure of souls" or discipline, but I will share insights chiefly regarding efforts of pastors to guide those who sought their counsel voluntarily. For it was the coercive aspect of discipline which eventually did it in. A major lesson to be learned from history, as a matter of fact, is that guidance can work only if it is voluntary, sought by the person receiving it.

As in so many other aspects of Christian practice, the apostle Paul developed a model that shaped the course of pastoral care. He established a paternal relationship with his converts and fathered them along, sometimes exercising sternness, at other times showing gentleness in order to get them to grow. "For though you have countless guides in Christ," he reminded the Corinthians, "you do not have many fathers; for in Christ Jesus I have begotten you through the gospel" (1 Cor. 4:15). What he tried to do for a whole congregation, he did with still greater care for special persons such as Timothy, whom he could call his "beloved and faithful child in the Lord" (1 Cor. 4:17) as well as his "brother" (2 Cor. 1:1; Col. 1:1; 1 Thess. 3:2). The first pastoral letters that have survived, whether by Paul or a Paulinist, gave spiritual as well as practical guidance under the names of Timothy and Titus. Judging by Paul's letters, he relied heavily on modeling in spiritual guidance. Over and over again he urged his charges to "imitate" him as he imitated Christ (1 Cor. 4:16; 11:1; 1 Thess. 1:6; 2:14). They were to have in them the mind of Christ (Phil. 2:5). It would be helpful if we could determine more precisely how Paul went about helping his converts develop "the mind of Christ," but he clearly expected the Spirit, the risen Christ, to guide them.

The truly innovative spiritual guides after the apostolic period were not pastors but teachers, particularly the Gnostics, including orthodox Gnostics like Clement and Origen. The Gnostic quest involved an ardent search for spiritual perfection. *Gnosis* meant to them not intellectual but rather spiritual knowledge. They aspired to go beyond the pedestrian level of ordinary Christian morality to the mystical realm, where they could experience in a momentary way the final goal of union with God.

Leaving aside Gnostics denounced as heretics, we find much of interest in Clement of Alexandria. Clement addressed his three major extant treatises to three different groups: *An Address to the Greeks* (or *Protrepticus*) to the unconverted, *The Instructor* (or *Paedagogus*) to ordinary believers, and *The Miscellanies* (or *Stromateis*) to persons who sought spiritual advancement. Clement was not complimentary toward those who said Christians ought to occupy themselves "with what is most necessary" and to ignore "what is beyond and superfluous."[1] Rather, he insisted, faith is a point of departure for *gnosis,* whose goal is a face-to-face vision of God. By practice of virtue the "gnostic" comes to resemble God as nearly as possible.[2] By withdrawing from sensual things and contemplating the spiritual, the gnostic imperceptibly moves closer to God and God draws nearer to him (or her).[3] Yet knowledge of God is gift. It is only by eminent grace, says Clement, "that the soul is winged, and soars, and is raised above the higher spheres, laying aside all that is heavy, and surrendering itself to its kindred element."[4] Such persons are alone qualified to serve as spiritual guides. The gnostic "fills the vacant place of the apostles by his [or her] upright life, his [or her] exact judgment, his [or her] assistance of the deserving, by removing mountains from the hearts of his [or her] neighbours and casting down the inequalities of their souls."[5]

So far as we know, Clement never functioned as a pastor, but Origen, his pupil and successor as head of the Alexandrian school, did. Ordained in Caesarea as a presbyter without the approval of his bishop, Origen spent the last years of his life, 232–254/55, in the Roman capital of Palestine. His sermons reveal a "gnostic" of the type which Clement described as trying to entice his flock to seek higher levels of commitment and understanding. According to his onetime student Gregory of Neocaesarea, the Wonderworker, Origen was a "spiritual guide" and "soul friend" in the true sense of these terms. Through study of philosophy, but especially of the Scriptures, he sought to inspire a love for the Word of God and the virtues that the Word could inculcate. He brought the pressures of friendship as well as those of scholarship to bear on this endeavor. Not surprisingly, Origen laid the foundations for monastic spirituality which would dominate Christian pastoral guidance throughout the Middle Ages. In his *Commentary on the Song of Songs* he set the pattern for the application of that writing to the interpretation of religious experience as a tryst between Christ and the individual soul. He also delineated the traditional stages of the mystical journey—purgation, illumination, and union.

From Origen until the Reformation, monasticism determined the character of spiritual guidance in the churches. The desert fathers, who began to appear in considerable numbers in the late third century, laid down the main guidelines. Had it not been for the efforts of bishops like Basil of Caesarea, their insights might have been lost. But the Rule, which he composed about 375, ameliorated excesses and made monastic guidance useful for the churches. Cassian of Marseilles brought many of the ideas of the Eastern monks westward. Through the influence of Augustine and Benedict of Nursia the monastic model dominated the pastoral office throughout the West. Gregory the Great's promotion of the Benedictine Rule assured it of a significant place in subsequent centuries.

Spiritual guides become known by being sought out by others, and hermits like Anthony, the so-called father of monasticism, attracted an army of admirers. Modestly educated themselves, they gave simple instructions for those who sought perfection in love, the vision of God, or the kingdom of God. The immediate goal, they taught, was purity of heart, for, according to Jesus' teaching, "the pure in heart" shall see God (Matt. 5:8). Monastic disciplines—solitude, silence, fasting, reading Scriptures, prayer, good deeds—were only aids in this endeavor; they should not sidetrack one from the principal aim. Nevertheless, the monks fashioned a variety of methods to attain the goal, and they passed these on to the clergy, many of whom came from the monastic ranks (often drafted forcibly into service).

By about 400, the monastic model had established itself as the model for the clergy. Bishops such as Augustine offered spiritual direction for both clergy and laypersons based on the monastic experiment. Augustine himself offered guidance ranging from elementary counseling of recent converts to advanced exchanges with mature persons such as Paulinus, bishop of Nola, and his wife, Therasia. From the latter he received as much as he gave. If Augustine's letters are in any way indicative of his personal approach, he had a finely turned sense of the guidance appropriate for a particular person. He was severe toward persons who played games with him, gentle toward those who were sincere, encouraging toward the despondent and fainthearted, provocative toward those who struggled to understand the Christian life. His occasional writings include numerous treatises composed to answer serious questions addressed to him by sincere seekers.

Monastic influences on the clergy notwithstanding, the real spiritual guides from Augustine's day onward were the monks, first the cloistered monks who furnished the cadre for most medieval churches and then, after about 1200, the mendicants —Franciscans and Dominicans—who traveled about offering guidance to the burgeoning number of those who felt disaffected or distant from the institutional churches. The Rule of Benedict, composed in 529, outlined a program of spiritual formation which clergy and laypersons, as well as "religious," could follow. It revolved around chanting the psalms eight times a day at stated hours interspersed with a regimen of work, study, and individual meditation. Within the monastery itself monks underwent thorough formation not merely in the understanding but also in the practice of the devout life according to Benedict's Rule. Normally a monastery functioned like a family, with the abbot at its head. But spiritual direction could be authoritarian, for one of the three vows that monks took was to obey superiors. Thus we know instances of extreme discipline of punishment meted out to those who violated some directive. But we should not frame a caricature based on extremes. Spiritual directors normally functioned like parents rather than like army generals or slave masters.

Bernard of Clairvaux (1090–1153) was the spiritual director par excellence in the twelfth century. Although he could be severe and inflexible toward "heretics" such as Peter Abelard, he based his direction of others on the conviction that love alone "can turn the heart from love of self and the world, and direct it to God alone. Neither fear nor love of self can turn the soul to God." He said in a letter to the Prior Guy and other religious of the Grande Chartreuse, "They may sometimes change the aspect or influence the actions of a man, but they will never change his heart."[6] Both sermons and letters reveal a guide who practiced what he preached and experienced.

By the end of the twelfth century the monastic monopoly on spiritual direction was slipping. Several factors account for that phenomenon: the alienation of masses from the church, the formation of sects which could meet better the needs of the masses, the transition from a predominantly agrarian to an urban society, and the corruption of the monastic orders themselves. Stepping into the role being vacated by the cloistered monks were the mendicant, or begging, orders, Franciscans and Dominicans and, later, numerous others. Instead of waiting for people to come to them, as the cloistered monks did, the mendicants went to the people. They preached, heard confessions, absolved sinners, and gave spiritual direction to all who sought it. It is scarcely surprising, then, that the popes would entrust to them the Inquisition, a program for revival and renewal of commitment, in 1232.

We would find little that was new about spiritual guidance by mendicants apart from the fact that it was now portable, and portability soon brought abuses and further disrepute for monastic models. It was not only Protestants who in the Reformation called attention to the abuses. A commission appointed in 1536 by Pope Paul III to study the need for reform of the church proposed in its *Plan for Reform of the Church,* which the pope later put on the *Index of Prohibited Books,* that cloistered monasteries be phased out because "many have become so deformed that they are a great scandal to the laity and do grave harm by their example" and that the appointment of friars as preachers and confessors be corrected.

The numerous sects that came into existence from about 1000 on repudiated the system of spiritual guidance framed by the medieval church in great part because of its authoritarianism. Oral confession in particular came under attack. The Protestant Reformers followed in the track laid by dissidents. Closing the monasteries and abandoning oral confession, they did away with virtually all of the paraphernalia of piety assembled to guide the faithful in the Middle Ages. The burden of spiritual direction now fell heavily on the Reformers themselves. Luther, for example, composed hundreds of letters of spiritual counsel, offering guidance in everything from prayer to practical problems of persons ranging all the way from Prince Philip of Hesse to barbers and farmers. Presumably he guided hundreds person to person. What fell by the wayside in Protestantism, however, was the availability of spiritual assistance for whoever would seek it. By the second generation the problem became acute, forcing the revival of many forms of medieval spirituality by Puritans in England and Pietists on the Continent.

Puritanism was spirituality. In their effort to effect a thorough reformation in England, equal to Calvin's in Geneva, Puritans resuscitated ascetic and contemplative practices of medieval monks—fasting, prayer, meditation on Scriptures, and all the rest. Like the monks, they coveted heart religion manifested in transformation of individual lives and society. Among the Puritans the clergy guided the faithful through preaching and through private means. On the Sabbath they gathered the specially devout in homes for extended discussion of the spiritual life, for prayer, or for inspiration. Pastors, like Cotton Mather, spent much time individually with those who sought special help, wrote letters of spiritual counsel, and did whatever they could to advance personal sanctity.

Pietism, a movement that caught some of its inspiration and character from Puritanism, used cell groups, or *collegia pietatis,* for spiritual guidance. Both laypersons and clergy gathered in these groups for Bible study, prayer, confession, and searching. Although the movement itself failed to outlive its two architects, Philipp Jakob Spener (d. 1705) and August Hermann Francke (d. 1727), it exerted a significant impact on Protestant spirituality through the Moravians, the Wesleys, and modern revivalism. The Moravian cell group furnished John Wesley with a model for the Methodist class meetings which offered corporate spiritual direction.

Unfortunately, the spiritual guidance that Puritanism and Pietism offered gradually succumbed under a variety of modern pressures. By the second generation the fervor of the first Puritans had waned and few sought the careful guidance of their forebears. Indeed, a "halfway covenant" had to be devised in order to allow many to exercise the rights of citizens, since the original covenant required faithful church attendance as a prerequisite. Meanwhile, the individual or group guidance of Pietism and the early Methodists yielded to the crowd mentality of revivalism from the Great Awakening of the eighteenth century onward. Many devout pastors doubtless guided numerous persons as they sought help, but personal spiritual guidance became increasingly casual and superficial as Protestant memories of earlier traditions in spiritual direction faded away.

In the Reformation and post-Reformation eras significant spiritual guidance has taken place chiefly in the Roman Catholic tradition. This happened because Roman Catholics reaffirmed at Trent the medieval models for which the Spanish revival had already opted. Ignatius Loyola fashioned a program of spiritual direction in his treatise *The Spiritual Exercises* which would dominate modern Catholic spirituality. Francis de Sales, bishop of Geneva, popularized the Ignatian approach in his *Introduction to the Devout Life,* written for a devout laywoman. At the heart of Ignatius' method lay his insistence on the absolute necessity of a spiritual director who would have more or less complete say over the person receiving guidance. The pattern of the devout life was to involve daily meditation, daily examination of conscience, weekly confession and communion, open confession to a good confessor, spiritual reading and fellowship with other Christians, and daily growth in virtues.

Space will not allow me to review the contributions of outstanding Catholic spiritual directors such as Teresa of Avila

(1515–1582), John of the Cross (1542–1591), Augustine Baker (1575–1641), Vincent de Paul (1576–1660), Jean Jacques Olier (1608–1657), François Fénelon (1651–1715), Jean Pierre de Caussade (1675–1751), Jean Nicolas Grou (1731–1803), on up to Thomas Merton (1915–1968). For the same reason, I must glide over Orthodox and Anglican traditions which have conserved many of the insights of the "catholic" tradition. You can read about these in Kenneth Leech's *Soul Friend* or Tilden Edwards' *Spiritual Friend*. What I must use the remaining space for is to present some constructive suggestions about the pastor as spiritual guide today.

The Pastor as Spiritual Guide

Because most pastors will hear what I am saying from the perspective of their training as pastoral counselors, I must briefly distinguish these roles. The chief difference would be that spiritual direction involves the direction of "healthy" as well as "sick" persons on a continuous basis, whereas counseling focuses on the emotionally distraught on a short-term basis. Although both director and counselor may employ similar methods, the former may focus more on the work of divine grace and bring to bear more of the resources of the body of Christ than the pastoral counselor. The latter's ministry, as a matter of course, tends to place emphasis on the individual rather than on the community.

Within the Protestant tradition I must emphasize the importance of voluntariness in spiritual guidance. To be authentic and responsible, obedience must be voluntary, uncoerced. If coerced, it is not obedience. The ease with which manipulation or coercion has often intruded on spiritual guidance, especially in relation to confession, is why Protestants have steered away from it or developed alternative means for sanctification. The cell group, for instance, has offered a more voluntarist mode of giving guidance. In instances where individual direction occurs, care should be taken to keep a voluntary covenant. Although the guide may exercise more explicit direction within this covenant, that too must be by consensus and not by coercion.

Here it is important for a pastor to remember that divine grace is the key in spirituality. We must not forget, therefore, the many channels through which spiritual guidance may occur, particularly the corporate ones. In the past, Protestants have sometimes overemphasized the individual and underemphasized the corporate means of grace. In our ecumenical era an increasing number of persons have learned to recognize the way in which sacraments or, above all, the church itself, as the *Ursakrament,* may channel grace. We must be careful not to restrict God's power in entering into human life and effecting change.

Pastors may guide others through carefully prepared for, planned, and executed public worship. Recital of God's mighty acts on behalf of humankind in Scripture, song, and prayer in itself offers the kind of direction many covet. We come to catch a vision of what God is doing in the midst of our lives and to share in a common experience of grace. Here, as in other facets of ministry, a pastor's personal preparation will have a weighty impact on leadership in this experience. A grace-filled person may help others find grace.

Pastors may also guide others through administration. Wayne Oates has taught many generations of students that pastoral care in its many dimensions depends on administration. An obvious structured means of spiritual guidance would be retreats or conferences set up for that purpose. Such retreats may take place in a variety of settings, but it is essential for most of us to withdraw from the clatter and busyness of our harried everyday lives to places of solitude and silence where we can spend time listening and being re-created by God. Retreat centers that have active communities of worship, most of which are Roman Catholic, provide more assistance in finding a spiritual path than those which supply only physical comforts and conveniences.

On a continuing basis pastors might offer spiritual direction through cell groups that would make spiritual growth their explicit goal. Within most congregations, Bible classes encourage, exhort, confront, counsel, and otherwise direct the faithful, but they seldom go far enough in doing so. Voluntary formation of groups for Bible study, discussion of Christian classics, meditation, or personal growth may be the best way to augment incentives built into the routine church programs. It is important here to combine the journey inward and the journey outward, because persons who turn in on themselves will become stunted. The most wholesome approach is one in which there is reciprocal interaction between four dimensions of spirituality—the social, the institutional, the intellectual, and the experiential.

The Church of the Saviour in Washington, D.C., is a good model to imitate. A major objective is to "call out the called." The members themselves assist one another in finding their "gifts" and exercising them by participation in groups toward which they feel a pull. The possibilities range from retreat and coffee house ministries to more activistic concerns such as peace-making, securing job opportunities, and refurbishing houses for low-income families. Social involvement may deepen spirituality even as spirituality may enhance social awareness. Pastors who are concerned for the growth of their flock, therefore, might use the strategy that Baron Friedrich von Hügel used with Evelyn Underhill when she came to him for spiritual direction. He instructed her first to spend two afternoons a week in the inner city among the poor. "You badly want de-intellectualizing or at least developing homely human sense and spirit dispositions and activities," he explained. If properly entered into, social service will "discipline, mortify, deepen and quiet you and distribute your blood—some of your blood—away from your brain, where too much is lodged at present."[7]

Wise pastors will also channel resources of others toward persons seeking spiritual guidance. Many of the finest guides are laypersons, ordinary saints who have spent hours in prayer and meditation, know the Scriptures, are sensitive to the human spirit, and, almost by instinct, point others in the right direction. Thomas Kelly spoke of "spiritual giants" whom he met in Germany in 1838 and who taught him deeper truths than he had gained through years of formal study. You may find some of these in every congregation.

Now, however, let us ask what the qualities of a spiritual guide should be. Kenneth Leech has drawn the following from a study of the history of spiritual direction. The first and most essential quality is *"holiness of life, closeness to God."* We can't guide others toward something we know nothing about ourselves. The second is *experience* of the realities of prayer and life itself. The third is *knowledge* of the Scriptures and the great writings on spiritual-ity. The fourth is *discernment,* perception, or insight into "the writing on the walls of the soul." The fifth is *submissiveness* to the Holy Spirit so that we may enable others to get in touch with the working of grace, with God.[8] Reflecting on these qualities, I would not encourage any pastor to set out to become a spiritual guide. That could lead to disappointment. Seek, rather, to be a person fully yielded to God, "God-blinded," as Thomas Kelly would say. If this happens, then other persons may seek you out as a spiritual friend, but it will always be presumptuous to assume you are such.

If someone should seek you out as a "soul friend," how would you go about guiding such a person? I would emphasize that rather than laying out a full-blown program, such as Tilden Edwards has outlined in *Spiritual Friend,* it is important that you be a good listener or have sensitivity to others. Douglas Steere has enumerated four qualities of such a listener, which I would call also the qualities of a good spiritual guide.[9]

The first is *vulnerability.* Vulnerability comes from the Latin words meaning "capable of being wounded." To be a spiritual guide to others, we must have a sense of our humanity. We will minister best to others as "the wounded healer," as Henri Nouwen has suggested in a book of that title. Or as the Puritan Richard Baxter put it, we will minister best as "dying men to dying men," "dying persons to dying persons."

The second is *acceptance.* Acceptance stands very near the essence of the Christian concept of agape love. Instead of attempting to shape other persons in our mold, we entrust them to the divine Lover. We accept them as they are, warts and all.

The third is *expectancy.* Expectancy is the product of Christian hope. In hope we uplift the other person. Douglas Steere has a gift for uplifting others. I have never been with him that I did not go away feeling uplifted. Reflecting on those meetings, I cannot attribute this to any particular thing he has said. Rather, it has something to do with his listening—with the sense of presence which he brings.

The fourth is *constancy.* Constancy means literally "standing with" or "staying with" the other person. Our tendency when we agonize through a long story with someone is to start ho-humming or to put words in that person's mouth. "Oh! You mean . . . " Of course, we know that person doesn't mean that. What we are saying is: "Why don't you say such and such and then we can get this review over with?" We have to stay with other persons, to struggle through with them.

Listening is more than hearing. We do not want only to grasp words, we want also to discover where words come from. We want to commune with the other person, to be united with the other.

In every conversation there will be more than the speaker and the hearer, more even than the one trying so desperately to communicate and the listener. There will also be the divine Listener, the divine Spectator—nearer to us than we are to ourselves. And if we are really listening, we may become the means through which another person breaks through, not just to another human being but to the Other.

A caution needs to be added here. Most persons who seek spiritual guidance will want to become spiritual giants overnight, and you may have the same aspiration for yourself as well as for the person you advise. I think it can be said without equivocation, on the basis of history and contemporary experience, that spiritual growth is seldom more rapid than physical growth. If we are serious about our relationship with God, we will be involved throughout our lives (and maybe even beyond) in a growth process. Those who assume they have achieved full stature are deceiving themselves.

In concluding, I would return to the point I made earlier concerning the pastor's role as a spiritual guide. The trick is to be a midwife or a mother of grace, to help other persons to discover the working of grace in their lives. A lot of methods may help in this ministry, but I would not encourage preoccupation with methods. More crucial is discernment, sensitivity to the Spirit's working in the life of another person. Discernment is given only to those who know the working of grace in their own lives. Let that endeavor, therefore, be the focus for your ministry. Who knows? Maybe you *will* add spiritual guidance to the many facets of your ministry.

3

Pastoral Care as Nurturing Spirituality in an Alien Culture

William E. Hulme

A few years ago, my wife and I took a hiking trip through the Welsh highlands, following the ancient pre-Christian footpaths. There were people in our group from all over Europe. During one of our breaks a woman from Austria, who was a reporter for her small-town newspaper, was telling of all the problems in her community. As a typical American I began to offer suggestions. After a while she grew impatient with my irrepressible helpfulness and said, "Oh, you Americans! You are always so optimistic! Don't you know that in Europe we are pessimistic?"

Our leader was listening to our conversation with amusement. Although an Englishman, he had lived in the United States for five years. He broke into the conversation and said to the woman, "You are right, Americans are optimistic. But in my observation of them they are only optimistic about tomorrow."

His words have stuck with me. He had zeroed in on a characteristic of our culture. If we are to nurture spirituality through our pastoral care, we will have to take into account the culture in which we in the United States live—a culture in which our optimism tends to be reserved until tomorrow. Our personal values, the quality of our living, the quality of our relationships

William E. Hulme is Professor of Pastoral Care and Counseling, Luther-Northwestern Theological Seminary, St. Paul, Minnesota.

and of our health, even our capacity for love, are inevitably influenced by these cultural priorities that press in upon us.

Gross National Product Mentality

Our culture is characterized by a gross national product mentality. We are a work-oriented, production-oriented, consumer-oriented, achievement-oriented, highly competitive people. Our emphasis is on striving. Not everybody has the advantages to enter the competition in such a society. Those who cannot, tend to become our losers. Loser is an awful word for us. Those who have the advantages to enter into competition in such a society find it difficult not to reflect in their lives this gross national product mentality. As someone has pointed out, it is indeed *gross*. It is hard on our health, an obstacle to our wholeness, and an impediment to our spiritual growth. Our focus, then, is on nurturing spirituality in the midst of these opposing forces in our culture.

Proving Our Worth

In the second letter to Timothy there are these words: "God did not give us a spirit of timidity but a spirit of power and love and self-control" (1:7). Rather than being self-controlled or self-directed, however, our experience is more that of being controlled, of being driven. "Driven," "compulsive," "obsessive" are frequently heard words in our culture and are all opposite of the word "free." They are psychological terms for what Paul called "the spirit of slavery" (Rom. 8:15).

To what are we driven? To establish our worth! According to our cultural values, our worth has to be proved. The pressure of this demand takes away the freedom we need to direct ourselves. Because our worth is at stake, we have an obsessive need for reassurance—"strokes." Because of this obsession, we have a need to please in order that we might be affirmed.

Running from Love

Under this pressure we easily become victims of the mirror image described in The Epistle of James: "He is like a man who observes his natural face in a mirror; for he observes himself and goes away and at once forgets what he was like" (1:23–24). James is referring to the mirror of the Word in which we see our total self, not just our physical appearance. We take a look, turn away and forget because we do not like what we see—a sight that threatens us with the painful experience of guilt.

This phenomenon has also been called the flush toilet syndrome. Since the advent of flush toilets, we think we can flush away the things we don't want to face—all symbols of rejection, all that is repugnant—and all is gone! This belief leads to a huge denial process which is basically a denial of our limits. Theologically speaking, this is a denial of our creatureliness, our mortality, our sinfulness. What we cannot face about ourselves becomes transformed into these compulsions and obsessions, which are the price we pay to perpetuate the illusion that it is gone.

The goal of our drivenness is not love as acceptance in which our negative qualities are realistically assessed, but rather love as approval which covers over the negative. Drivenness is basically a running. A running from what? Ironically, we run from love (love as agape) as unconditional acceptance to love as adulation in which we are praised for our achievements—our works. This seeking for love as adulation results in a strong need to please, which leads to a dependency on strokes.

Now, strokes are nice to receive, for we all want them and need them. Since this is the case, we should be more ready to give them. At the same time, one can experience a famine of strokes. Many of the persons to whom we give care and counsel are experiencing such a famine. We pastors can experience these famines also. Then what? How does one endure, survive, if one is dependent on strokes for such endurance?

Predisposition to Addiction

Our ability to carry on when we are running from real love depends on a tenuous balance of conflicting forces within us. This predisposition leads to some form of addiction. We need something to capture our attention; otherwise we may take a look into that threatening mirror. It is no coincidence that a culture with the values and priorities of ours should have also a gigantic problem with addiction.

Addicts are running from life, from themselves as they are. The most common of our addictions is to alcohol, with its astronomical cost to our economy, our national health, and the welfare of our families. While no respecter of class or station in life, alcoholism carries with it a social stigma.

There are also nonchemical addictions. One of the most common of these is television. This addiction particularly afflicts children, as the family television set may be on for six or seven hours a day. Through this addiction there is a lot of brainwashing and reinforcing of passivity. One of the television channels in our community—to its credit—offered families dialed at random from the phone book $500 to turn off their sets for a month. As a television repairman took out the sets from each home—the channel didn't trust the families—he said it was "like a death in the family." This experiment became the title of the report that was televised also by public television on the "Bill Moyers' Journal." The statement reminded me of what Billy Carter was reported to have said when he gave up alcohol: "It's like losing my best friend." Many of the families experienced withdrawal symptoms similar to those of drug addiction.

Another nonchemical addiction is work. In contrast to alcoholism, work addiction has a social honor associated with it. We need to distinguish between workaholics and hard workers. Hard workers are those who find in their work an outlet for their creative energies. They work hard at it and receive satisfaction from doing it well. This is the dignity of work. Those who have work that provides them with such a challenge are indeed fortunate.

Workaholics also work hard but as though their very self-worth depended on it. And in the workaholic's mind-set, it does. Workaholics are attempting to prove or establish their worth through their work. Their addiction is to a never-ending quest for an illusional reward.

The opposite of workaholics are the "sluffer-offers." They also believe that succeeding in one's circle is the way to self-worth, but they don't believe they can do it. So rather than investing themselves into this route, they protect themselves from the judgment of not making it by doing as little as they can in order to get by. As a result, they can reassure themselves that they ought not to be judged, because they did not put themselves into it. They are like the college student, whom many of us remember, who shouted in the dormitory hall the night before the big final test, "Who wants to go with me to a show?" Such students are on record that they are not investing themselves in the test. And so, how they do is no indication of whether or not they have what it takes. Who would ever put himself or herself on the line by shouting in those same halls, "I'm putting everything I have into this test"? Judgment would be too threatening to one's sense of worth.

Some addictions are more harmful than others. Alcoholism seems to be the most harmful in terms of its effect on human life; work addiction is perhaps the least harmful. But we are not sure. There has not been enough research into the potential damage to health, family relationships, or spiritual growth as the result of workaholism.

An addict's narrow focus causes him or her to lose sight of other values. In alcoholism we speak of a loss of control—of self-direction. The first step of AA is a confession: "Our lives have become unmanageable." Why? Because they are possessed by addiction—a compulsion or an obsession. In addiction, a *means*—alcohol or work—is converted into an *end*. That which is a means for enjoyment or a means for accomplishment becomes the end-all of life. Such a substitution is one definition of idolatry. In work addiction, for example, the goals of accomplishment, achievement, and progress are so transient in satisfaction that striving for them actually becomes satisfaction. Here is the source for the reservation of our optimism until tomorrow. We are striving for it today.

The Need for Scarcity

This focus of satisfaction on striving itself is illustrated by the familiar analogy of the ox on the treadmill. With the carrot hanging in front of his nose, the ox believes that he will ultimately reach it by walking toward it, when actually he is walking on a wheel. If the ox ever caught on, the whole operation of the mill would stop. Perhaps this picture is where we get the expression "stupid ox!" But is the ox any more stupid than a human being on a symbolic treadmill pursuing a symbolic carrot?

Striving on the treadmill depends on, thrives on, scarcity. The things we want, the time we need, the affection we desire are all scarce because they *need* to be scarce. It is hard to tolerate abundance. Who has enough time? Yet when we get an unexpected block of time—such as when delayed or waiting—we may feel anything but good about it. In fact, we may become murderous in our intent and contemplate how we can *kill* time. Imagine—killing the very time we supposedly cannot get enough of.

In our culture we give money as a reason for working. Not needing the money can be frightening, since we use its scarcity to justify our working. Actually, our work may be that which is holding us together. Losing this "glue" is one factor in the problems of retirement. What takes the place of work? Money is a more acceptable reason in our culture for work than less materialistic reasons. This reasoning contributes to the relatively low status of volunteer work.

We all desire affection. Yet if it comes in abundance, it can frighten us. We might even draw back from it. We fear intimacy as well as desire it because it threatens to take away the safety we have in distance.

So we see that abundance actually becomes a problem. An abundance of time can prove boring. More money means there is never enough. Although affection is a potential of most moments, it may be seldom expressed. So it is that God is much more willing to give than we are able to receive. The ministry of pastoral care and counseling cannot give anything to its recipients. What it can do is assist persons to remove the obstacles within themselves that are preventing them from receiving the grace that abounds.

Sexual Energy and Work

Our cultural values and priorities fashion a life-style that is hard on our intimate relationships such as marriage, family, and friendships. They cause one to ration what does not need to be rationed. Take affection, for example. It is scarce because we may be putting most of our sexual energy, our affection and passion, into our work.

When we think of sex in our culture, we think almost exclusively of sexual intercourse. This view is a distortion by a culture obsessed with sex. Sex as sexual intercourse is a focused view of sex. There is a broader, more diffuse view. From this broader standpoint, sex is inseparable from our personhood. It affects all that we are, think, feel, or do—for God created us as sexual beings. Sex is involved in our outreach to others—our warmth, our caring, our affection. It is shown in the hug, the kiss, the arm around, the touch. The bumper sticker "Have you hugged your child today?" is right on. We could put it in theological terms and say, "Have you incarnated your love for your child today?" Have you given it flesh and blood?

Sex is involved in our love for the beautiful—the beautiful scene, art, music, our appreciation for rhythm. It is expressed in our activities—our work, the creativity and passion we put into it. It is expressed in our religious faith. Our hymns are frequently erotic in their imagery: "Jesus, lover of my soul, let me to thy bosom fly." Our worship is affectional as it climaxes in the Lord's Supper in which the unconditional care of God is communicated in conjunction with a caring family of God around the table. In receiving the intangible through the tangible—Christ's body and blood through the bread and the cup—we can perceive God's touch in the Lord's Supper. Christian fellowship is a further example of sexual expression. We have not yet achieved the New Testament practice of "greeting one another with holy kiss." Some of our congregations are "passing the peace." For some people, however, this touching is an ordeal and they stiffen in reaction to this generous overture of affection.

Obviously our sexual energy is expressed in sexual intercourse. But it is also expressed in intimacy at broader levels as we enjoy the warmth, affection, the closeness of our cherished personal relationships. In fact, sexual intercourse between a husband and wife, Christianly speaking, is a celebration of a loving, affectionate, and committed relationship.

Our creative and sexual energy goes also into our work. It belongs there, enhancing the dignity of work. There is less guilt, however, when we invest this energy in our work, since the work ethic of our culture supports such a choice. So we can overinvest in work, which then is expected to meet too many of our needs —needs it was never meant to meet. Of necessity, work begins to absorb most of our energy. What results is the starvation of our intimate relationships and the upsetting of the balance in our lives. In the pastoral care of families we are continually confronted by this deprivation of intimacy and imbalance in living. Our problems of time distribution may be reflections of a deeper problem, the distribution of personal energy.

The "Until" Syndrome

How does this imbalance affect the quality of our lives, our mental and physical health, our spirituality, or even the caliber of our work? We have in our community a clergyperson who works as a community organizer for a grass-roots community organization. I asked him to speak to my seminary students on the subject of community organization, since a pastor has a community in the congregation and it functions much better for ministry when it is organized than when disorganized. I gave him an hour, and after a half hour he had spoken about only organizing one's self. I felt I had to interrupt while there was time or the students would have been unhappy over his not having dealt with the announced topic. "Bob," I said, "pardon me, but our time is half over and we need to focus on the subject." "What subject?" he asked. "How to organize a community," I replied. "We *are* on it," he said. "You can't organize anybody else until you can organize yourself. I'm on step A; I'll get to step B, but first let me lay a good foundation." I got the point.

The subject of organizing ourselves leads us to the question of our priorities and values. This question may force us back to the mirror. Who decides for this person before the mirror? Whose expectations is he or she trying to live up to? Whose identity is really there? It is so easy to project the responsibility for the answer to these questions on our environment and present ourselves as victims of circumstance. This projection is our resistance to taking responsibility for who we are.

Such resistance is due largely to our resistance to limits. As those "in the flesh," we can have insatiable egos and chafe at the limits of our creatureliness. This pattern is behind much of our drivenness. As a consequence, we develop the "until" syndrome: Until things change "out there," don't expect them to change "in here." The old song, "When the work's all done in the fall," expressed this projected optimism. Then things will change. At our seminary we say, "When this quarter is over." Pastors may say, "When this Christmas season is over, then things will be different." So, when this project, this program, this drive, this press is over, then we'll live the kind of lives we really want to live.

In contrast to this "until" syndrome, the Scripture focuses on the present: "Behold, now is the acceptable time; behold, now is the day of salvation" (2 Cor. 6:2). It is a chronic cop-out when change is continuously focused on the future, for then it rarely, if ever, takes place. Instead, we make some pacifying rearrangements to satisfy pressures—from the family or from the physician. But no change takes place in essence, values, priorities, or basic drivenness. We have done what Jesus warned us against. We have taken the new garment and instead of putting it on and becoming new, we have cut it up into pieces to patch the old. There is no exorcism of the "spirit of slavery," no putting on the new.

Struggling as a Game

The saving reality is that we have conflict—a conflict over the way things are. It persists as a protest, though feeble. The focus on striving for a nebulous tomorrow is not a way of life that brings satisfaction. The carrot teases, or frightens, or disappoints. What it can't do is *satisfy*.

The conflict may precipitate a struggle. There is ambivalence, double-mindedness. A businessman shared with me his frustration over his unsuccessful efforts to live out his own moral convictions. He was an addict, not to alcohol, nor to television, not even to work. He was addicted to sexual promiscuity. Evidently I was not showing sufficient empathy, because he stopped in the middle of a sentence and pointing to me said, "You don't know the struggle that goes with each of my falls." No, I didn't. But I knew now why he was continuing to fall. With whom was he struggling? The devil? According to the New Testament, if we resist the devil, he will flee from us (James 4:7). As the hymn says, "One little word shall fell him." "Get behind me, Satan!" (Matt. 16:23). Actually, he was struggling with *himself*. He was "feeding" both sides of his struggle. What kind of game is this?

Struggling is necessary when we are confronted with a difficult decision. When it is difficult to know what is right or wise or appropriate, when the area is gray, we struggle with the issue so we can make the best possible decision. On the other hand, struggling can also be a game we play to *avoid* making a decision. This man knew what was right; so over what was the struggle?

Struggling implies that one is attempting to make a decision. Actually, it may be a way of neutralizing the protest or pacifying the consequence. We play the game, "Look how hard I'm trying," like those who use confession as a substitute for changing. They are still not disposed to look into the mirror, to see what is going on, to glimpse not only weakness but *duplicity*. Struggling may be a sign of how tough the decision is, but the struggle itself is no substitute for the decision, no compensation for a fall.

No struggle is recorded in the way Jesus dealt with his temptations in the wilderness. While we have only a brief focus of that experience, we obviously have what the Evangelists considered the main import. The issue was clear: "Jesus said, 'It is written.' " The result was clarity of decision. Turn the stone into bread and satisfy your hunger. He said, "It is written, 'Man shall not live by bread alone, but by every word that proceeds from the mouth of God.' " Cast yourself down from the Temple and get an instant following. "It is written, 'You shall not tempt the Lord your God.' " Fall down and worship the devil and fulfill the popular conception of Messiah. "It is written, 'You shall worship the Lord your God and him only shall you serve' " (Matt. 4: 1–11).

Struggling, as a game to avoid making a decision, has its effects, but they are all negative. It is hard on our self-esteem; it undercuts our self-direction; it cuts into the efficiency of our old nature but produces no change to the new. It does not prevent our sinning, it only prevents, as Luther said, our sinning *bravely*. It predisposes life to be cyclical—going in circles or wandering in the wilderness.

Called to Be Faithful

We need to give and receive permission to stop the struggle —the game we play with ourselves. We are called of God to this end. There is an almost frightening simplicity to decision—that carrying out our power of choice. We need to face the reality of our freedom, the freedom we have, under God, to change. As Paul says, "For freedom Christ has set us free" (Gal. 5:1). Therefore, use it!

An important function of people in the helping professions is to facilitate this permission to leave the old—one's destructive ways—and to offer the support and inspiration for the courage needed to enter the new and constructive. In pastoral care and counseling, this function is understood as facilitating a response to God's call to grow.

We are called to be faithful stewards to what God has given us, such as twenty-four hours a day. It is ironic that it took someone who was terminally ill with cancer to found a life-giving movement called Make Today Count. Orville Kelly, in 1973, was given the diagnosis of inoperable cancer. There was little that medical science could do for him. He was a relatively young man with a young family. His wife knew of his condition, but his children did not. For a couple of weeks Kelly was depressed and the atmosphere in the home was tense. The children knew something was wrong but didn't know what. Kelly decided with his wife to tell them. Calling them together, he informed them of his condition, telling them that he probably would not be with them for long, but that he wanted what time he had to be a good time. He would have his good days and his bad days, but he wanted to make every day count. To do this he needed their help. So they covenanted together as a family to make every day count.

This covenant so revolutionized his family living that he wrote an article about it for his Burlington, Iowa, newspaper. Soon he began to get calls and letters from the terminally ill and the families of the terminally ill asking more about making today count. Once I was scheduled to hear him, but he had to cancel out because it was one of his bad days. A year before he died in 1982, a friend of mine heard him speak. When asked to reflect on the years that he had cancer, Kelly said, "I wouldn't wish my cancer on anybody, but if I had to choose a life without cancer or my cancer and the meaning of life which has come since then, I would choose the cancer."

During the latter part of his illness Kelly also founded another organization, the National Association of Atomic Veterans. Kelly believed that he contracted his cancer as a United States soldier assigned to the atomic bomb testing program. Along with others he was told to enter the radiated aftermath of the explosions for investigative purposes, being assured there was no danger. Now we know there was. Shortly before he died, he won his first class-action suit. From Kelly's experience it would seem that the quality of living may be one factor in quantity of living. In a sense, we are all terminal. Today is the day that needs to count.

We are all called to be faithful stewards of the gifts of love and affection and also faithful stewards of the gifts of enjoyment of creation. Faithful means full of faith. Faith gives us the courage to see, to look into the mirror, to identify with whom and what we see there—and to accept whom we see there. Søren Kierkegaard said that if we are to move from the spot where we are, we must begin at the spot where we are. God's acceptance of us in Christ gives us the power to begin at the spot where we are as the only way to move from the spot. God's forgiveness permits us to be realistic and positive at the same time. We are sinners and at the same time justified. Being both realistic and positive is the needed combination to bring about change. If we are simply realistic, we may have a legitimate cause for becoming depressed. On the other hand, if we are simply positive and not realistic, we are under an illusion, and sooner or later we will crash against the hard ground of reality. What enables us to deal with reality positively is the faith that sees in, with, and under the present moment of negativity the hidden presence of God. The result is hope.

The good news that undergirds this hope is that our worth is a gift, sealed in our baptismal covenant. This gift from God contradicts the cultural assumption that our worth must be proved, and provides freedom from bondage to this pressure. This freeing gift is an emancipation for which people in our culture are longing. It is the focus for our pastoral care as spiritual nurture in an alien culture.

Faith also gives us the freedom to imagine, to picture, and to implement our decisions. A look in the mirror is not a fixed stare. The perception goes beyond *being* to *becoming*. We have the vision of what the Spirit can do in the lives of those who are reconciled to God. This vision is a second mirror: "The fruit of the Spirit is love, joy, peace, patience, kindness, goodness, faithfulness, gentleness, and self-control" (Gal. 5:22–23). We can take the leap of faith and visualize these possibilities for ourselves in the mirror of promise. We can hear the call of God to see it, for God wills our sanctification, our growth in spirituality (1 Thess. 4:3).

From Defeatism to Victory

We have the freedom through forgiveness to move from defeatism to victory—a movement described in Romans 7 and 8. Whoever put the chapter division in the midst of this dramatic description did us a disservice. Romans 7 and 8 are of one piece, for the descent to the depths in Romans 7 leads to the ascent to the heights in Romans 8.

Defeats can be preludes to victories and not just more defeats. We can learn a lot from them, providing we are reconciled with them. Otherwise we tend to repeat them. So we need to face and feel Romans 7, the mirror of defeat, the judgment of the law. The good that I would, I do not, and the evil that I would not, I do. We face and feel our helplessness—but also our duplicity. For the good that I would is also the good that I would not, and the evil that I would not is also the evil that I would. So the existential agony: "Wretched [person] that I am! Who will deliver me from this body of death?" (Rom. 7:24).

Then we catch the vision of Romans 8. Who shall deliver? The answer is inherent in the question. "Thanks be to God through Jesus Christ our Lord!" (7:25). Then follows the ecstasy. "There is therefore now no condemnation for those who are in Christ Jesus" (8:1). "For I am sure that neither death, nor life, nor angels, nor principalities, nor things present, nor things to come, nor powers, nor height, nor depth, nor anything else in all creation, will be able to separate us from the love of God in Christ Jesus our Lord" (8:38–39). "No, in all these things we are more than conquerors through him who loved us" (8:37). We can feel the ecstasy, experience the resurrection.

Each moment is not only *chronos* but *kairos*. Chronos is time as quantity measured by minutes, hours, and days, but *kairos* is time as quality in which something new can enter our personal history. As *kairos*, the present moment is not simply the inheritor of the past, but is itself the opportunity for a fresh start. Being open to this possibility in every moment is what is meant by the receptivity of faith. In the words of Romans 8, "If the Spirit of him who raised Jesus from the dead dwells in you, he who raised Christ Jesus from the dead will give life to your mortal bodies also through his Spirit which dwells in you" (8:11). We *have* good news. It is our resource in our pastoral care as spiritual nurturers in an alien culture.

4
The Power
of Spiritual Language
in Self-understanding
Wayne E. Oates

In the Yahwist's earthy and unblushing account of the Creation, we do not have to rack our brains to grasp what the author is getting at. We are shown a simple but exquisitely tender picture of God himself leading animals to the man and waiting expectantly to see what he would name them (Gen. 2:19). The gift of the *ability* to speak, to use language to *name* the animals, symbolized the man's power over them. The power to name animals is only the beginning. We are given the ability to name actions and thoughts with verbs and ideas, to put our feelings into words and pictures. In the process of doing so, we make decisions as to who we are, to whom we belong, what we are doing, and where we are going in life. We make covenants, we break covenants, and we remember covenants with the words we have used to describe them.

Language, therefore, is powerful as we walk in the garden of life in the cool of the day and try to hide from God or as we confess our sins to each other and to God in order that we may be healed (Gen. 3:8). Language is also the mechanism of confusion as we compete with each other in building Towers of Ambition, destroying the unity of a "whole earth" with "one language

Wayne E. Oates is Professor of Psychiatry and Behavioral Sciences, Director of the Program in Ethics and Pastoral Counseling, University of Louisville Medical School, and Senior Professor of Pastoral Care, Southern Baptist Theological Seminary, Louisville, Kentucky.

and few words" (Gen. 11:1). The Lord God confuses the language given to us. He scatters us over the face of the earth. We leave off building because we do not understand each other's speech (Gen. 11:7–8).

In this volume devoted to the state of the art of the pastoral care of the sick and the well, the broken and the whole, those who mourn and those who celebrate, I want to focus on the power of language—both verbal and nonverbal—to heal and to hurt, to break apart and to bind together, to comfort and to condemn, to celebrate and to make jealous. Language energizes our self-understanding. We do these ministries in a world that is confused. Strident rhetoric struts in its masquerade of understanding. We do not have a common international language, a common interchurch language, nor a common interprofessional and interdisciplinary language. We are not a world with "one language and few words" (Gen. 11:1).

Historically, our task as pastors, therefore, has been and will continue to be one of translation and interpretation as we help persons, as Charles Gerkin says, to grasp and put into effect the intention of God in the long sweeps of persons' life stories. We are, he says, "listeners and interpreters of stories."[1] This requires language, a common language at that. Consensual validation in speech calls for a meeting of meaning in words. John Wycliffe (1320?–1384) determined to translate the Latin Vulgate into the English tongue for use by the common people. He began the process of providing a common language for the English people. Before his time they spoke a far larger number of different dialects than afterward. William Caxton (1422?–1491) translated French stories about Troy, Aesop's fables, and Cicero. He set up his own press and published Chaucer's *Canterbury Tales.* Before he could do so, however, he decided for himself what precisely "he meant by the 'English language,' for there were almost as many languages as there were countries in England."[2] Then came the King James Version of the Bible, which, as Daniel Boorstin, the Librarian of Congress, says, shaped and invigorated the English language. He also says the King James Version is perhaps the only literary masterpiece ever written by a committee. Shakespeare (1564–1616) wrote his major works in the same period. The powerful spirituality of these shapers of the English language gave English-speaking persons a common identity, an awareness of selfhood, and a means of communion and commerce with and concern for each other.

This heritage has been ours as Americans. The power of biblical and Shakespearean English has been our means of understanding ourselves and each other until the middle of this century. The wholesale branding of spiritual language as unintelligible God talk, the increasing secularization of American education, the severing of technological education from the humanities, and the intensive specialization of professional education—particularly theological, medical, and legal education—however, have shattered the English language itself into as many dialects of sophistication in the helping professions as there were dialects in England before Wycliffe's translation, Caxton's work, the King James Bible, and Shakespeare's writings. We are a people "without one language and few words." We leave off building a common self-understanding of our spiritual selfhood, of our healing in time of suffering, and our redemption in the face of our mortality and death.

Therefore, you and I as theologian-pastors once again face the responsibility of translating the dialects of the secularized value systems of the behavioral sciences into the wisdom, words, and power of the good news of God in Jesus Christ. This translation is not quid pro quo, tit-for-tat rendering. For example, psychologists and psychiatrists, such as Erich Fromm, make much of self-love as the measure of the love of others. They occasionally think to quote Jesus as a teacher of this idea. So he was. But that is not the highest measure of love of others that Jesus taught. He said, "Greater love has no [person] than this, that a [person] lay down his [or her] life for [a] friend" (John 15:13). Furthermore, he said, "A new commandment I give to you, . . . even as I have loved you, that you also love one another" (John 13:34). Every good translation has a built-in interpretation that is true to the things-in-themselves being translated. Therefore, the Christian pastor who disciplines himself or herself has as much to share with as to receive from the psychologist and the psychiatrist.

In order to make concrete what I have said thus far I want to take the concepts of temptation and sin, as we perceive them in the Judeo-Christian Scriptures, and translate them back and forth with psychological and psychiatric concepts of unacceptable and socially maladaptive human behavior. Doing so has specific rewards for you and me as pastors of persons who disburden to us their complaints before God.

For as Luther said, one reason Protestants are opposed to the Catholic confessional is that they don't *want* to make confession. But as Calvin commented, "Let every believer, therefore, remember that if in private he is so agonised and afflicted by sin that he cannot obtain relief without the aid of others, it is his duty not to neglect the remedy which God provides for him—viz., to have recourse to a private confession to his own pastor." He further says that "confession of this kind ought to be free so as not to be exacted of all, but recommended to those who feel that they have need of it."[3] Such a translation gives us a larger repertoire of responses to persons for whom the "shorthand of grace" is a closed book, as Scott Peck calls the great Christian words of reconciliation, redemption, and sanctification. For many respond to these words as the "same old stuff," as clichés that we say because we are supposed to say them. A wider choice of idiom has more chances of being heard.

Furthermore, such translation helps us to work more effectively with other professionals in our mutual care of persons. At the same time, we can establish a spiritual community with them, many of whom were reared in the Judeo-Christian faith but have been amputated from it by the confined straitlacedness of family, home churches, and synagogues, and by the secular humanism of their educations. The choicest reward, however, is that pastor, parishioner, psychologist, and psychiatrist have new access to the power of spiritual language in our understanding of ourselves and each other. Thus, we can more faithfully do the works of love toward each other in a common language of the grace of God in Christ.

Temptation

First, let us attempt a translation of the Christian understanding of temptation. We of the Free Church tradition—Baptists, Methodists, Disciples, etc.—have equated temptation with sin. However, Jesus was tempted in all points as we are, yet without sin. So—there must be a difference between the two. Yet in conventional wisdom the thoughts of anger, lust, or envy are the same as the acts. Dietrich Bonhoeffer says that "temptation is a concrete happening that juts out in the course of life."[4] Temptation, however, is a universally human experience either ignored or misinterpreted.

Temptation as Defense Mechanism

The psychologist and the psychiatrist have largely secularized the modern understanding of temptation with their elaborate descriptions of the defense mechanisms of projection, reaction formation, and fantasy formation. Projection is seeing our own faults in others rather than ourselves. It is overtaking a brother or a sister in fault *without* looking to ourselves lest we are also being tempted. Reaction formation is the "Mr. or Ms. Clean" syndrome of vigorously acting one way in order to keep from doing just the opposite. Nietzsche described it when he said our contempt is the sidelong glance of our envy. Shakespeare put it well when he said, "[He] doth protest too much, methinks." Jesus put it best when he spoke of blind guides who strain at gnats and swallow camels (Matt. 23:24).

Fantasy formations get at one of the major themes of temptation in Christian teaching. Fantasy formation, psychiatrically speaking, is a mental substitute for action, a dreaming state while awake, the high imagination, for example, that one is now a king and then a slave, that one is exempt from death, that one is in total control of everything one wishes to control, or that one is an exception to all rules of life, both old and new. These childish feelings of omnipotence "sicklied o'er" the path of action "with the pale cast of thought," as Shakespeare described it. One does not actually sin, but only thinks about what it would be like to do so. Thus he or she becomes what Nietzsche again called the "pale criminals" who, he said, "possess their virtue in order to live long in a miserable ease."[5]

Jesus' word "blind" describes precisely these thought processes of projection, reaction formation, and fantasy formation. The person does not know consciously what he or she is up to. Yet these processes use up energy just the same and can "burst open," as Kierkegaard was fond of saying, into mindless and bizarre actions which only lamely deserve the name of being good, clean, honest sin. They are blind and unconsciously driven actions. They are the state of sin "couching at the door," as God said to Cain. "Why are you angry, and why has your countenance fallen? If you do well, will you not be accepted? And if you do not do well, sin is couching at the door; its desire is for you, but you must master it" (Gen. 4:6–7). Self-understanding comes from *knowing* what you are thinking and doing what you purpose to do under God, not being drawn blindly by your unknown fantasies. As Socrates prayed, "O Lord, give me beauty in the inner person, and may the outward person and the inward person be at one." Only God can really bring this to pass. The psalmist's prayer says it best: "I hate them with perfect hatred; I count them my enemies. Search me, O God, and know my heart! Try me and know my thoughts! And see if there be any wicked way in me, and lead me in the way everlasting!" (Ps. 139:22–24).

Temptation as Response to Abandonment

Yet these are not the most life-threatening conceptions of temptation shared in the different languages of the Christian faith and contemporary psychiatry. The most lethal disorder with which psychiatrists deal is clinical depression. The person so afflicted often dies by suicide. The person is clutched by a dreadful unspeakableness, an overpowering sense of being helpless in the face of the terror of his or her desolate orphanhood in a cold, gray, relentless world of no options for living. Often such persons will tell us that God has forsaken them, that the Spirit has left them, and that they have committed or are about to commit the unpardonable sin. One such man, when I asked him what his greatest temptation was, said, "To kill my whole family and myself."

Dietrich Bonhoeffer is the great translator of this understanding of temptation into the language of the Christian faith. He says:

This is the decisive fact in the temptation of the Christian, that he is *abandoned,* abandoned by all his powers—indeed, attacked by them —abandoned by everybody, abandoned by God himself. His heart shakes, and has fallen into complete darkness. He himself is nothing. The enemy is everything.[6]

Bonhoeffer quotes Psalm 38:10: "My heart throbs, my strength fails me; and the light of my eyes—it also has gone from me." Yet the saving insight he quotes from Isaiah 54:7–8, 10:

> For a brief moment I forsook you, but with great compassion I will gather you. In overflowing wrath for a moment I hid my face from you, but with everlasting love I will have compassion on you, says the Lord, your Redeemer. . . . For the mountains may depart and the hills be removed, but my steadfast love shall not depart from you, and my covenant of peace shall not be removed, says the Lord, who has compassion on you.

You and I are on pilgrimages of self-understanding as we exist before God; we seek to know ourselves even as we are known of God. This knowing can best be achieved by turning whatever cleverness we have inward upon ourselves. Along with the sense of humor that can laugh at ourselves, this cleverness helps us to face with courage our own fantasies and dark feelings of having been abandoned. Our own temptations are the obstacle course and drill field in which we learn, both biblically and psychologically, terms to discern reality, to represent reality, and to bring an inseparable comradeship to those who feel abandoned by people and by God. Thus God becomes good news to us and makes us good news to others.

Sin

Most of what psychiatrists and psychologists have to say about guilt refers to the experience of temptation, not sin. Sin is a relational and not just an intrapsychic experience. Sin is estrangement from God and from our neighbor, for whom we are responsible before God. David had sinned against Uriah, Bathsheba, and his child by Bathsheba who died at its seventh day. Yet he prayed to God: "Against thee and thee only have I sinned." His primary separation was from God. Yet, for the sin against Uriah, Bathsheba, and his son he felt acutely responsible to God. Karl Menninger asks, whatever happened to sin? One thing that happened was the exclusion of God from our sense of responsibility for our actions. Secularization does just that. The secular sciences, however, still have humanistic assessments of human behavior which, when put into relationship to God, become translatable into Judeo-Christian concepts of sin. Let us examine several, not all, of these psychiatric and psychological assessments.

Complexes

Carl Jung speaks of this independent action of a part of the psyche against the total person as complexes. He says, "The . . . complexes . . . come and go as they please. . . . They have split off from consciousness and lead a separate existence . . . being at all times ready to hinder or reinforce the conscious intentions."[7] Andras Angyal calls these "part processes" of the human spirit. They are to him "bionegativities" with the power to rule the whole life.

Plato said that sin is a rising up of a part of the soul against the whole. Treating the total person was Hippocrates' way of being a physician. The Judeo-Christian tradition teaches that the life is in the blood, that revelation comes through the normal processes of the human body, and truth is incarnated in human flesh of prophets and ultimately of Jesus of Nazareth. Illness results when any part of the whole organism begins to eat away at all the rest of the organism with no regard to its own place in the totality of the person's being. Plato did not call it illness. He called it sin, the violation of the whole by the part.

Jesus used a surgical metaphor to drive home the truth of the part against the whole of our beings. In one of the most difficult passages in Jesus' teachings, he said:

> If your right eye is your undoing, tear it out and fling it away; it is better for you to lose one part of your body than for the whole of it to be thrown into hell. And if your right hand is your undoing, cut it off and fling it away; it is better for you to lose one part of your body than for the whole of it to go to hell (Matt. 5:29–30, NEB).

This metaphor is essentially a surgical figure of speech referring to the domination of the whole life by a sexual maniac. Surgery is recommended. It is better to cut out sex than to be a sexual maniac. Anyone working in a rape relief center will nod her head yes. Some even justify male castration as a treatment. The psychotic patient likewise reads this text concretely, literally. He or she actually does pluck out the eyes or cut off the hand. One psychiatric contribution to the Christian perception of sin is the way persons avoid the larger issue of consecrating our sexual energies to God and the responsible care of the sexual partner by becoming overconcrete and literal about figures of speech. Jesus did mention straining gnats and swallowing camels. Paul did say that the letter kills but the Spirit gives life (2 Cor. 3:6). Hence, sheer peril accompanies being too allegorical, metaphorical, or symbolic with psychiatric patients. This particular passage from the New Testament can be deadly to some. When I hear a psychotic patient quoting it, I know the person will literally gouge out the eyes or cut off the hands if given a chance.

Sin as That Which Is Unfitting

In the classical Greek world, people had a verb, *dikaioō,* which indicated an attachment to what is fitting, right, fair, or orderly. The opposite was *adikeō,* which meant to do wrong. The adjective *dikaios* meant observant of customs, well-ordered, and civilized. The Greeks' almost inerrant sense of line, proportion, symmetry, and beauty inheres in this concept. Psychiatric assessment today uses it regularly to identify what is appropriate and inappropriate, fitting and unfitting, in place and out of place. The common populace is much more harsh on inappropriate behavior than upon infractions of the Ten Commandments.

The apostle Paul uses this concept of observing customs, of acting appropriately about the eating of meat offered to idols. In Romans 14:14 he says, "I know and am persuaded in the Lord Jesus that nothing is unclean in itself; but it is unclean for any one who thinks it unclean." In 1 Corinthians 10:23 he says, " 'All things are lawful,' but not all things are helpful . . . not all things build up." He put the principle of appropriateness into the larger ethical context of "building up" one's neighbor, being empathetic toward his or her sensibilities. Thereby he made simple, appropriate behavior an exercise in reverence for one's neighbor and for God.

Sin as Cowardice, Shrinking Back, Refusing to Grow

The developmental perspective of redemption and sin is both corporately and individually evident in the history of the Old and

New Testament peoples. The psychological and psychiatric interpretations of health and illness stand on the understanding of persons either growing or regressing. These interpretations are translated to give a fresh approach to the life of love and faith before God.

The process of growth in different levels of maturity being put away in behalf of a higher one is the meaning of love in the Old and the New Testament. Children drink milk; adults eat meat (Heb. 5:11–14). When you are a child, you think and act as a child; when you are an adult, you put away childish things (1 Cor. 13:11). You are to put away the elementary things of the faith and "go on to maturity." Not to do so is sin. To do so takes faith. "Whatever does not proceed from faith is sin" (Rom. 14:23). The opposite of sin is not purity, perfection, or "compulsive, obsessional, nasty niceness," as Paul Adams so vividly puts it. The essence of sin is shrinking back, losing one's nerve, refusing to grow. These picture phrases are nonlegalistic conceptions of sin as the failure of nerve in the face of the demands of maturity. Faith is the courage to grow. As the writer to the Hebrews says, "Do not throw away your confidence, which has a great reward. . . . We are not of those who shrink back and are destroyed, but of those who have faith and keep their souls" (Heb. 10:35, 39).

Sin as Impaired Judgment

One of the concerns of the psychiatrist in assessing a patient's mental status is the quality of judgment the patient demonstrates. Is it impulsive, with no regard for time? Is it grandiose? Is it self-derogatory, resulting in self-immolating behaviors?

The conception of sin from classical Judaism and Christianity that is relevant here is that of "the fool." *Nabal* is the empty person. *Saral* is the thickheaded person. *Kesil* is the boastful, overconfident person most often mentioned in Ecclesiastes and Proverbs. In the New Testament the *anoëtes* is the thoughtless person. The unwise person is the *asophos*. The *aphrōn* is the headless person (Thou fool . . .). The *mōros* is the slow of heart and dull-witted. These are all persons who are presumed to have average or above-average intelligence that they are not using. The feebleminded, the mentally retarded, are called *oligopsychos* and are to be treated tenderly and with compassion.

The Judeo-Christian classical tradition of sin lays great emphasis upon the use of the intelligence, for the mind of man is the candle of the Lord to be used with diligence, reverence, teachableness, and care. In pastoral care you may be asked, "Do you think what I am about to do is good or bad?" You can say, "I would prefer to ask, 'Is it wise or unwise? What kind of wisdom does each alternative have? In short, is this or that action foolish? Which has the most sense? God gave you good intelligence and foresight; how do you use these gifts in this situation?' "

Sin as the Bondage of the Law

The revolt of the New Testament era, led by Jesus of Nazareth, was sparked by the excessive weight of the bondage of religious control, ritual, and ethical hypocrisy. The law of Moses was initially devised for the health, ordering, and well-being of persons. Much of it was built around sheer survival needs in the austere desert country of Palestine and the Sinai Peninsula. Contrary to eras of the past, such as those of Josiah, Isaiah, Jeremiah, Ezekiel, and others, no real internal reform was even in the distant future. Religion became a compulsive binding force that was rigidly enforced by a theocratic hierarchy. Some religious authorities exercised both religious and political force in the lives of people. The kind of ritual blindness of which Freud spoke in late nineteenth- and early twentieth-century Vienna was mild in contrast to it. Little wonder is it that Harry Emerson Fosdick said that what Freud called religion Jesus called sin.

This weight was bound upon the people by the ecclesiastical power figures. Jesus said that these power figures lived in kings' houses and wore soft raiment. They bound heavy burdens and did not lift a finger to help people bear them. Religion was a business, not even a form of entertainment, as, for the same reasons, it often is today. Jesus invited people who were outcasts to come to him. He extended forgiveness, love, acceptance, and healing to them. He said, "Come to me, all whose work is hard, whose load is heavy; and I will give you relief. Bend your necks to my yoke, and learn from me. . . . For my yoke is good to bear, my load is light" (Matt. 11:28–30, NEB).

The yoke of which he spoke was not a day's work for bread to eat. It was the demand of professional religionists that was destroying their lives. It was the same yoke of which Paul spoke to the Galatians. He had taught them a way of life that revealed God as a God of unconditional acceptance, love, and forgiveness. He had taught them that redemption which comes from faith of a person who is willing to learn, to grow, to change into a mature person. They wanted to go back to the new moons, sabbaths, the rules, the regulations, the compulsive security operations of their past. He said, "For freedom Christ has set us free; stand fast therefore, and do not submit again to a yoke of slavery" (Gal. 5:1).

Yet the raison d'être for having a serious rather than a perfunctory approach to pastoral counseling in the care of the psychiatric patient today is that about 17 percent of our patient population suffers from this kind of bondage to a life-threatening kind of religious burden. Our task is to use things both old and new from our good treasure to make faith in Christ a source of power, not a legalistic reinforcement of the sick religion on which they have been reared. Psychiatrists and ministers are at the point now of ceasing to write about whatever became of sin and starting to ask whatever became of forgiveness and creative refusal to give up on people.

Sin as Idolatry

Another classical conception of sin relevant to the care of psychiatric patients is that of sin as idolatry. Psychiatry, however, has no valid equivalent for the translation of idolatry into a therapeutic sense. The very idea of idols implies the criterion of the one true God. A *purely* secular professional represses the idea of the Transcendent into his or her unconsciousness. This is not to say that all professionals are purely secular. Many are highly informed religious believers. Here, however, is where the Judeo-Christian faith has a basic contribution to make. A patient or a physician does not believe in God, let us say. Then we must ask, "What *kind* of God is it that you do not trust or believe?"

Paul Tillich defined idolatry well when he called it absolutizing the relative. Any relative value, person, cause, possession, or such can take on absolute value to a person. Such people feel that without this particular value their world ends, they cease to be a person, they are a "zero," they do not exist. Persons who have invested all their emotional resources in a spouse fall apart when death, divorce, or defection takes that person from them. Persons whose work is the sum total of their existence tend toward suicide when they find themselves in an unbearable cul-de-sac on that particular job. Parents whose world orbits around a particular son or daughter soon find that they themselves are a vital part of the son's or daughter's real pathology. In such instances they, for all practical purposes, are idolaters.

I spoke several years ago with a woman whose marriage had collapsed in divorce. I asked her if her husband had been an idol to her. Her reply the next day was that her husband had not become an idol but that the institution of marriage had, and without the status of being married, she was a nonperson, her life had no validity, she did not want to live. One can see a tiny shaft of light as to what was wrong with the marriage. A husband is more than a means to keep an institution of marriage intact; certainly a wife is. Marriage, like the Sabbath, was made for persons and not persons for the marriage.

Therefore, pastoral counseling is somewhat iconoclastic, especially when psychiatric categories become burdens laid upon the backs of persons, with no one to lift a finger to help them bear them. These categories we use can easily become a yoke of bondage, just as other religious rituals and prescriptions. They can become vested interests of power, idols in themselves. They can prompt the necessity for a return again and again of a Spirit that offers a yoke that is easy and a burden that is light, a faith imbued with joy.

Sin as Self-elevation and the Destruction of Creation

Another profound concept of sin is self-elevation, hubris, and its consequent assumption that you or I are to take God's place. It, too, finds little conceptual base in the behavioral sciences. Here again the Christian can make a contribution to the behavioral sciences. The alienation of persons from God comes by their intention to put themselves in God's place. Erich Fromm provides us with a historical study of this in his book *You Shall*

Be as Gods. The philosophical grasp of the meaning of the demonic is right here. In the Promethean will, man steals fire from heaven and is excommunicated. Lucifer pulls a power play in heaven and is thrown from among the gods. Nietzsche was most honest about it: "There is no god. If there were, how could I stand it if I were not he?"

The critical issue in this concept of sin, however, is not that an individual tries to be God, although unwillingness to live within, understand, and enjoy the limits of being human is one way to go mad. The critical issue is when ways of life are developed which assume that we as creatures know better how our bodies personally and corporately can live than does the Creator. Thus we put pollutants into our bodies that shorten our lives. We use time, energy, and relationships in ways that doom us to failure. We develop an energy policy and insist on selling multimillions of cars to use more gasoline. The creation is diverted, perverted, converted, and reverted away from its original aim. Such is our self-elevation.

Sin as Missing the Mark

A most common meaning of sin is simply that of missing the mark—bad aim, low shot, cheap shot, poor shot, missing the mark. Behavioral sciences give little attention to psychological equivalents for this idea. "The mark" here has a backward and a forward meaning. We miss the mark of the intention of God in creation and therefore are alienated from ourselves and others, as well as from God. We miss the mark of our own sense of calling and destiny and therefore lose our way and sense of direction in life. Helen Merrill Lynd calls this kind of feeling *shame* in her book *Shame and Identity.* Therefore, we as therapeutic agents of healing find that the forgiveness of sins and the restitution of creation joins hands with the healing of the total being of the person.

Thomas Merton describes missing the mark and hitting the mark well in his metaphor: "A tree gives glory to God by being a tree. For being what God means it to be, it is obeying God. It consents, so to speak, to God's creative love. It is expressing an idea which is God's and which is not distinct in essence from God, and therefore imitates God by being a tree."

Sin as Violation of a Covenant with God

One biblical understanding of sin has no translatable equivalent in the behavioral sciences that I can find; that is the transgression of an individual or small group within a fellowship of persons against the covenant that binds them together. A covenant is the spiritual vision and shared responsibility of a community for and to one another and to God. A covenant is a solemn promise before God made binding by a commitment in words and ritual symbolic acts. Christians are bound together by the new covenant of Christ's blood. The Lord's Supper is the ethical threshing floor for our motives either in tune with the covenant or in violation of the covenant.

Christian marriage is built upon such a covenant, and this covenant is not to be a nonverbal covenant and certainly not a set of blind assumptions. To develop a shared wording of this covenant is the purpose of premarital counseling, wedding ceremonies, and marital counseling. Trust is vested in the keeping of these covenants. Distrust, suspicion, and alienation arise when they are broken. The covenant itself has a separate existence of its own as a regulator and interpreter of behavior. Sin is a violation of the substance and intent of these covenants. Keeping faith becomes the criterion of integrity, health, hope, and growth. Breaking the covenant becomes the measure of sin.

For this conception of sin, only the anthropologists and the experts in primitive psychiatry give us any inkling. Yet their discussions are, it seems to me, "arms distance" discussions. The scientist *studies* these things but does not include them in their own treatment plans. They are more or less curios and museum pieces that pique the curiosity but do not affect the practice of therapy.

In this sense, the Christian community can be admonished to take itself more seriously and to be more articulate and redemptive in the exercise of its covenantal nature. Even among us as Christians, however, we ourselves have become so fragmented and secularized that *we* too are unconscious of our covenantal nature as we address the sins of the world.

Secular and sacred believers alike, we and the behavioral scientists stand together as sinners before whatever God we perceive as our ultimate concern in our loss of awareness of our essential covenantal nature as human beings in relation to each other. Alan Paton, in his poignant novel about South Africa, has a way to describe us. Writing about a dramatic moment in the life of a South African tribe, he says:

> Kumalo began to pray regularly in this church for the restoration of Ndotsheni. But he knew that was not enough. Somewhere down here upon the earth men must come together, think something, do something. . . . For who would be chief over this desolation? It was a thing the white man had done, knocked these chiefs down, and put them up again, to hold the pieces together. But the white men had taken most of the pieces away. . . . He looked at the counsellors . . . and he saw too that they were frowning and perplexed, and that for this matter there was no counsel that they could give at all. For the counsellors of a broken tribe have counsel for many things, but none for the matter of a broken tribe.[8]

And neither do we.

5

The New Language
of Pastoral Counseling

John Patton

For some time now, psychotherapeutic psychology and psychiatry have been developing a new language. Although learning the details of that language is important for only a few of us, understanding the reason for its development is important for most of us because a comparable situation and rationale exist within the field of pastoral care and counseling.

The *Diagnostic and Statistical Manual of Mental Disorders,* published by the American Psychiatric Association,[1] has been revised to provide for a broader range of descriptive categories more inclusive of social and situational factors in a person's life. The new system tells us more about what people are like rather than simply teaching us how to fit them into categories. Whereas Freud believed that any hope for credibility rested upon his ability to theorize in terms of physical science, Heinz Kohut, probably the most widely influential figure in recent psychoanalytic thought, has presented his work in terms of a new epistemology of empathy—knowing and theorizing based on the intuitive clinical knowledge of the analyst rather than that of an objective external observer.[2] Another psychological theorist, Roy Schafer, has endeavored to develop a theory out of the knowledge of practice—one that is closer to human experienc-

John Patton is Executive Director, Georgia Association for Pastoral Care, Atlanta, Georgia.

ing. Schafer describes his project as "developing an action language . . . by means of which psychoanalysts may hope to speak simply, systematically, non-mechanistically of human activities in general and of the psychoanalytic relationship and its therapeutic effects in particular."[3]

What I am suggesting by pointing to these phenomena in psychiatry and psychoanalysis is that the psychological sciences seem to be aware of a literalism or fundamentalism within their field of endeavor and are attempting to move toward new theories that are closer to human experiencing. I believe that pastoral counseling, at this point in its history, needs to do a similar thing and that our heritage from persons like Wayne Oates calls us to do just that.

I have been discussing psychological issues also because Wayne Oates and my teacher, Seward Hiltner, made it both possible and relevant to discuss openly the contributions of psychological knowledge within a forum on ministry. I was not alone in my assumption, in the early 1950s, that to use psychological knowledge in any professional sense I had to become a psychologist as well as a minister. Oates and Hiltner taught us that this was not the case. Psychological knowledge and experience not only can, but must, be used in the service of ministry and theology.

A more important part of our heritage from the fathers in our field is psychological, but not primarily that. It is an awareness of a different kind of pastoral authority—an authority of relationship based upon what a pastor is and understands about persons within his or her care. It is an authority which demonstrates that we do not have to tell persons what to do in order to minister to them. I have not counted the books that Wayne Oates has written. I believe, however, that more important than what is said in his books has been what he has attempted to personify in all his work—namely, that we learn pastoral care and counseling through experiencing and reflecting upon the caring relationship. His attention to the central reality of how I care and am cared for has been the appropriate focus of our heritage in pastoral care and counseling for the past thirty-five years.

The purpose of the new language of psychiatry has been to break the bondage of old categories and move closer to human experiencing. Kohut is seeking to honor Freud by avoiding a fundamentalism of Freudian categories. His theoretical work grew out of the reality that psychoanalytic theory was not broad enough to fit his work with patients. He was convinced that a larger group of patients could profit from analysis than suggested by the theory. He sought, therefore, to develop a theory more in keeping with his practice. Moreover, he insisted that practice also offered a way of *knowing* that had not been adequately recognized as a valid means of acquiring theoretical knowledge. Empathy, for Kohut, was not as much offering warmth as providing skilled professional understanding of the patient gained through relationship. Thus Kohut's work reaffirms the value of clinical knowledge for theoretical formulation.

Although focusing upon somewhat different issues, Roy Schafer's work also calls psychoanalysis back to its practice. In that practice, he says, psychoanalysis does not view a person as a victim of forces within, as a rigid interpretation of Freud's metapsychology implies, but as an actor in life, doing things that are ultimately understandable and meaningful.[4] Parts of the theory must be changed to fit the best in clinical practice.

In pastoral care and counseling we honor our fathers, not by speaking the same language they spoke, but by addressing the issues of today and tomorrow in ways as relevant and useful as theirs have been. My concern here is to suggest for pastoral counseling a language that can avoid our own fundamentalisms of (1) substituting words for reality and (2) substituting ways of thinking about relationships for the vitality of the pastoral relationship itself. My thesis is that *pastoral counseling involves both a deepening of one's experience of life and faith and the learning of new ways of sharing that experience in relationship.* An appropriate language for understanding and sharing experience is neither psychology nor theology, although it is psychological and theological. It is a "close-to-experience" language which is clinical, mediating, and relational.

Pastoral Counseling's Clinical Language

Several years ago, during the fiftieth anniversary year of Clinical Pastoral Education, I found myself imaging a reunion of the family of *Clinical* and *Pastoral* with the conversation common to such gatherings as to who looks more like which side of the family. My identification of the clinical side of the clinical-pastoral "marriage" still seems to me to be a satisfactory one. *Clinical,* as we understand it in our field, is the "direct, first-hand involvement in the world of persons, in contrast to the second-hand *knowledge about* provided by interpretive materials, such as books or lectures. It refers to experiential knowledge of the stuff of life, particularly interpersonal life."[5] If the goal of pastoral counseling is the deepening of one's experience of life and faith through relationship, I believe that the language of pastoral counseling must continue to be a clinical language.

For me that means, most importantly, the language of the client or parishioner. It means the best of what I learned at the University of Chicago Counseling Center—trying to enter the frame of reference of another person. There may indeed be limits to this mode of interpersonal encounter, but the problem for most of us is that we have not learned it well enough. In his major theoretical statement on personality theory, Carl Rogers defined empathy as being able

> to perceive the internal frame of reference of another with accuracy, and with the emotional components and meanings which pertain thereto, as if one were the other person, but without ever losing the "as if" condition. Thus it means to sense the hurt or the pleasure of another as he senses it, and to perceive the causes thereof as he perceives them, but without ever losing the recognition that it is *as if* I were hurt or pleased, etc. If this "as if" quality is lost, then the state is one of identification.[6]

Empathy, for Rogers, is the primary way that we know, and its direction may turn inward or outward. It involves both feeling with (being vulnerable to suffering) and seeing with (having the capacity to see as the other sees or as my deeper self sees). The first thing we have tried to teach students in clinical training is the kind of empathy that both Rogers and Kohut describe. It involves feeling with, that is, searching out the feelings of another and helping that person focus upon and be in touch with the affective dimension of life. The caricature of the Rogerian "you feel" is an amusing part of our heritage, but helping persons experience and share their feelings is one of the most important parts of pastoral counseling.

Scientific methodology, for Rogers, is not so much a way of

knowing as "a way of preventing me from deceiving myself in regard to my creatively formed subjective hunches which have developed out of the relationship between me and my material."[7] We know through these subjective hunches, experientially, empathetically, or phenomenologically (through involvement rather than through detachment). Rogers's view of empathy is often thought to be only an uncritical warmth toward the client. In actuality, although the theoretical framework is different, Rogers and Kohut share a very similar view of clinical knowing through empathy.

The "new language" of this knowing is the language of symbol and story—a language that facilitates the perceptual dimension of empathy. If we are to see as another sees, then we must find ways to help that person share the pictures and stories of what their lives have been. "I was the last one chosen whenever there was a game." "I was the cheerleader who tried to stir up others, but never knew what I was feeling." "My mother never liked me, but she made good tuna fish sandwiches." All of these images enable us to see as others see. They also get us out of the realm of abstractions into the stuff of life so that we can know from our own experiencing.

To hear someone say that he always feels left out is understandable, but not directly experienceable. To say "I was the last one chosen," however, allows me to see, hear, and touch what that is like. Either it happened to me or I can remember my feelings when it happened to another. I can therefore feel what the other is feeling through feeling what I feel. I can go with that person to one particular place in his or her pilgrimage rather than being lost in generalizations that avoid reexperiencing what it was like. Being clinical is helping persons deepen their experience of life through immersion with them in the uniqueness of their life experience—being able to value it in a way that may have been lost by the clients or parishioners themselves.

For ten years or so we have had as a part of our advanced CPE program what has been referred to by the students as "Patton's Storytelling Seminar." When we began the seminar I thought of it as a corrective to the sometimes overanalytic process of CPE that may erroneously suggest that ministry is primarily dealing with the psychodynamics of another person. In that seminar students have been required to write brief narratives of their present life (something that happened during the last week), stories of the past, and fantasies of the future. Later in the process they write stories of patients to whom they are trying to minister. In the seminar we attempt not to critique a person's style, but let our imaginations respond to the pictures created by the story. The most common result of the seminar is a sense of the rich uniqueness of human life and experience and being able to carry away a "picture" of fellow students and patients. The obvious value of this expanded awareness for pastoral counseling is the way in which image and story enable pastors to appreciate the person seeking help as more than a type of problem that they should know how to solve.

To be a clinician means to be more involved in doing it than thinking or writing about it. Our heritage in pastoral counseling and clinical pastoral education calls us to remain interested in the "living human document." Charles Gerkin has recently used that phrase from Anton Boisen to title his book on a hermeneutical theory of pastoral counseling.[8] Although I prefer more relational images to describe ministry and feel that his hermeneutical theory may overemphasize the importance of words, Gerkin's book is a valuable resource for the new language of pastoral counseling. A statement by Karl Menninger can offer a useful caution to anyone who may place too much value on what he or she has to say to another:

> Interpretation is a rather presumptuous term. . . . I dislike the word because it gives young analysts the wrong idea about their main function. They need to be reminded that they are not oracles, not wizards, not linguists, not detectives, not great wise men, who like Joseph and Daniel, "interpret" dreams—but quiet observers, listeners, and occasionally commentators.[9]

Given this caution about the potential grandiosity and distancing quality of the image of the interpreter, clinical language does require continued attention to the way in which we attempt to explore life's meanings with our clients and parishioners. In this connection I have been influenced by an article on "Interpretation as Devotion"[10] which appeared in *The Psychoanalytic Review*. In that article, Susan Handelman brings an important insight to Protestant Christians, although that is not her major purpose, about the contribution of the rabbinic tradition to our thinking about life.

> Freud may not have liked being classified with the Talmudists, but as he admitted, the uniqueness of his approach to the dream and his success in revealing its secret . . . was that he treated it as Holy Writ —like a Rabbi—searching for hidden significance in every word and detail.

Handelman notes that in the Jewish tradition, text and interpretation are inseparable. As in Freud, the interpretation is the completion and complementary elaboration of the dream.

> The interpreter stands in a passive-aggressive role, engaged and detached, determined by and determining the associations and thoughts of the unconscious, which ultimately lead to the mysterious unknown, beyond reason, explanation, and understanding. . . . Both the psychoanalyst and the Rabbi assume a hidden meaning, which in its manifestation is multiple—and not so much found in the text as a reified essence, but *in* the process of interpretation.

For the rabbis, Handelman continues, "interpretation was not a provisional prelude to a final 'pure' understanding (as it was for the Christians) but part of the divine revelation itself. . . . 'Remember' is the theme that permeates both the Bible and Jewish history."

This view of interpretation seems to be a valuable corrective to the view that what we are about in life is to find the truth as quickly as possible and then hold on to it with all our might. That posture is one of the things that most interferes with the process of pastoral counseling. In contrast, what seems to me to be most important in pastoral counseling is to invite a person to explore and share with me what it has been like to live his or her life. The words of Binx Bolling, the twenty-nine-year-old stockbroker who narrates Walker Percy's first novel, *The Moviegoer,* suggest in another way what is facilitated by pastoral counseling:

> The search is what anyone would undertake if he were not sunk in the everydayness of his own life. . . . To become aware of the possibility of the search is to be onto something. Not to be onto something is to be in despair.[11]

The forty-year-old single woman who comes to me because she must have a hysterectomy and feels that, as she puts it, she "missed it all" needs to have me respond sensitively to her feelings of grief and loss of a part of her life just as Rogers taught me to do. She also needs, even in the very first session, to have me respond to something more than her pain and begin to see and talk about the story of her life. My task as a pastor is to try to find a way to put her "problem" in the perspective of her whole life and suggest that what she might do with me is to explore her life as well as her problem. The primary value of pastoral diagnosis is not to find out what someone has, but to find ways to explore what they are and may become. That is the beginning of the kind of search that may lead one out of despair.

It is also a way of acquainting persons with their likeness to others. The most useful statement of clinical wisdom I have ever encountered is Harry Stack Sullivan's "We are all more alike than otherwise." Most of what is best in pastoral counseling can be seen as assisting persons to discover the gospel in that statement. The function of diagnostic knowledge for both pastoral counselor and counselee is revealing how each is both like as well as different from everyone else.

To minister to a person who appears to have signs of severe mental illness, we need to have enough psychological knowledge to refer that person to other types of care. Even here, however, helping someone see his or her humanness as well as illness is an important contribution of the pastor. A client of mine has said, jokingly I think, that all I have taught him in the time he has been coming to see me is that he is sad and not depressed. Pastoral counseling understood that way is indeed a language game. If so, however, it is an important game. For what I think I have been doing is to offer the good news to my client that his sadness is ultimately like yours and mine and thus he is not really alone as he has always thought. That is another way in which pastoral care is clinical.

Pastoral Counseling's Mediating Language

The language of pastoral counseling is neither theology nor psychology, although it is theological and psychological. One of the important implications of being clinical—being fully immersed in the human situation of the persons to whom I attempt to minister—is that I cannot simply translate my client's life situation into either theological or pyschological terminology, although I am constantly tempted to do so. I have been so educated in psychological diagnosis that when my counselee says that he doesn't enjoy sex very much because it is wet and noisy, I may delight in having found an old-fashioned obsessive-compulsive neurotic in a world of narcissistic and borderline personalities. My job as a pastoral counselor, however, is to stay with the close-to-experience language of his life supplemented by my own commonsense language rather than classifying him and teaching him the classification. My example may seem like too much of a caricature, but one of the unfortunate aspects of some of our training in pastoral counseling is that we have taught students a lot of psychological language that they do not know how to use.

The problem of theological language may be even more acute. As one committed to the importance of Christian theological meaning, I find it difficult not to place the case with which I am dealing immediately within that framework and feel satisfied that I have done so. For example, I am presently studying the problem of human forgiveness as I see it in pastoral counseling. When I hear someone say in a counseling interview, "I don't believe that I can ever forgive him," it is virtually impossible for me not to be thinking, "I know how you can do it" or, "You're lucky to have come to me." My commitment to the clinical prevents me from verbalizing any of these statements even though I feel that I have insight into the Christian "answer" to the problem. It is not that my "answer" is unimportant or that I am afraid to make a Christian witness. It is, rather, that I believe the language of pastoral counseling is to be a mediating language between theology and human experience rather than one that consistently uses theological terminology.

One reason for this reserve is that using theological language with a person requires either membership in the same religious community or some agreement on the part of the counselee that he or she wants to think of life in Christian theological terms. I recall with delight years ago when I first read some of Paul Tillich's theology. According to my understanding, Tillich's dealing with the problem of faith and doubt presented the unbeliever struggling with his unbelief as one grasped by the unconditional—a faithful person through his doubting. When I pointed out this idea to a skeptical young professor at the university where I was a campus pastor, he informed me in no uncertain terms that he did not want to be made a believer without his consent. I decided that even though it helped me to think of him in that way, I had better keep it to myself and find other ways to talk to him.

Another issue in the use of theological language in pastoral counseling is timing. In an editorial in *The Journal of Pastoral Care* I told the story of a young woman who, after several months of counseling, said to me tearfully, "Why didn't you tell me when I first came to you that I was morally and spiritually bankrupt?"[12] I said to her as I would say now, "It takes time to develop a language to talk about things like that." Although a parish minister and a member of his or her congregation are members of the same religious community, it is quite different to speak theologically in a pastoral conversation than it is from the pulpit. From the pulpit the preacher says in effect, "He who has ears let him hear," and the hearer has the freedom to apply the message to his or her situation or ignore it. In talking to an individual or a family, a "community" of conversation about faith is developed in relation to the particular struggle of those unique parishioners or counselees. It is their particular situation that must be addressed, not the human situation in general. The pastor must know some of these particular dimensions of the faith of those persons in order to relate it to the faith of the church.

What, then, is this mediating, in-between language? Paul Pruyser in *The Minister as Diagnostician* provides an excellent example. His diagnostic variables offer important suggestions about the kinds of things that pastors should be discussing with people. They present a language that is both psychological and theological but that is not identified with any particular psychology or theology. Pastors need to be more comfortable in that in-between field of psychology of religion than they usually are, because the appropriate subjects of discussion in pastoral counseling are religion (understood psychologically in terms of a particular person's or family's faith) and psychology (understood as the psychology of that particular person or family) viewed from the point of view of religion. When he speaks of our needing to be comfortable talking about an awareness of the holy, the sense of providence, the capacity to hope, gratefulness, the sense of responsibility and repentance, communion or kinship with others, and the sense of vocation,[13] Pruyser is calling us to a discussion of the important phenomena of human life, not to theology or psychology as such.

Over the past few months a couple have been coming to see me, presenting a problem described initially as the wife's depression and their difficulties in communicating. Several years ago, when she was still a teenager and he in his early twenties, they "saved" each other from the drug culture of a large Midwestern city by getting "saved" in a conservative Bible church. Since they have been in the Atlanta area, however, he has become successful as a salesman, while she has been at home with their child. They have not found a church that fits either their history or their present reality. Marie is upset about Marvin's anger around the house, his moodiness, and his insensitivity to her and others. She tries to recall him to the time when religion had helped them and talks to him about "the Lord." Marvin tells me that he's into "the Lord" but not twenty-four hours a day. She shares with me her desire to do what is right and her struggle with being "submissive" to Marvin. My work with them involves sharing their pain, as any good parent might do, and teaching them to talk deeply with me and with each other in language that is respectful of what it meant to them to be saved, yet one that is related to the life they lead now and to what salvation might be like in the present. They are similar to the psalmist, who really does not know whether or not he can sing the Lord's song in a strange land. I am trying to teach them some new words for the strange land in which they now live.

One of my favorite essays by Seward Hiltner appears in the 1960 report of the Association of Seminary Professors in the Practical Fields and is entitled "Implications for the Ministry of the Dialogue Between Doctrine and Experience." I suppose I particularly like that essay because Hiltner describes the dialogue between doctrine and experience using a clinical report of mine that described the ambiguity of an evangelistic call. In commenting on that call, he wrote:

> The student felt, upon due reflection, and I believe rightly, that his reflection on all this, systematically carried out, had illuminated for him certain aspects of the relationship of faith and works in the

Christian life. Reflection on ministerial experience had led not only to practical insights but also to a new apprehension of basic dimensions of Christian doctrine.[14]

I have been using this essay with students for years, attempting to encourage them to think theologically in the light of their experience in ministry. My efforts, however, have been only partially successful. But I have been unwilling to surrender the thesis that pastoral experience can contribute significantly to doctrinal insight and that clinicians can think theologically along with the more academically oriented. My attempts to interpret these data have led me to conclude that a step in the process has been left out. The theological reflections at the end of verbatims from CPE have generally been inadequate because we have tried to force them or insist that the student have a theological insight as soon as he or she writes up the pastoral experience.

What has gone wrong is that we have not taken Hiltner's words, "upon due reflection," seriously enough. Perhaps he did not, either. Theological reflection, as my colleague Zeke Delozier has helped me understand about pastoral consultation, is like manure. It has to age before it does much more than smell. Delozier insists that a period of time pass before students formulate their reflections upon either personal consultation or theology. This time of reflection prevents the kind of off-the-cuff sloppiness that one can so often see in so-called experiential theology which is born out of pastoral experience.

What happens during the period of "due reflection," or while the manure ages, is that one uses his or her imagination. In our particular training program we use the "storytelling" seminar to help cultivate the imagination. Reflection that uses the imagination is an insufficiently recognized step in theological construction, even though its importance has been emphasized by theologians like Ray Hart and Theodore Jennings.[15] It is that step which asks us to take a pastoral experience that has been "meaning-full" and not "do anything" with it for a while. Let the crucible of faith, both within one's own life experience and within the community of faith of which one is a part, make its impact upon the experience. Then one can begin to suggest how the experience provides a particular insight into doctrinal theology. In the light of what one's imagination has done during the step between experience and doctrine, how does pastoral experience contribute to the formulation of one's faith?

For example, one experience that is constantly impacting my work in pastoral counseling is the way in which persons talk about being right, or in the right, when they have been hurt by someone close to them. A man reflects painfully with me about his wife's infidelity, but in trying to talk about his own life he moves quickly away from the pain to his righteousness—telling me how different he is from his wife and how his relationships with other women have always been natural and innocent. After the interview, my imagination begins with what I have heard and then wanders. The phrase comes to mind: *when being right seems wrong.* Although it sounds like a sermon title—and some of the fruits of the imagination can appropriately be used in that way —what my imagination is doing is continuing to reflect upon the pain of this man and some of the paradoxical ways that right and wrong seem to be expressed in his life. My conviction is that he is beginning to teach me something about the meaning of righteousness in the Christian life—what it is and isn't. I make notes on these impressions, remember things I have read and heard, allow other experiences to come to mind, and someday—I hope before too long—I will attempt to make some statement about the Christian life in the light of this pastoral experience. The language of pastoral counseling is a mediating, close-to-experience language of the imagination, some of which may be shared with the client or parishioner, much of which will only be used to sensitize me to both my theology and my practice of ministry.

Pastoral Counseling's Relational Language

Perhaps the most important thing about the language of pastoral counseling is its awareness of the limits of language. As important as it is to speak in a language that is clinical, or close to experience, and one that mediates between that experience and the words of our faith, our heritage in the pastoral care movement of the last thirty-five years reminds us of the limits of words. What you say is important, but not most important. There is authority in presence as well as in word. The traditional understanding of ordained ministry as being one of Word and Sacrament can remind us that if even *the* Word is not adequate without the word-transcending reality of Sacrament, how much less are even the best of our words and stories.

We have learned some of the significant lessons about the limits of our words through pastoral care's heritage in crisis ministry. One of the most important things that CPE has been able to teach pastors is to keep their mouths shut—at least some of the time. I used to have a guideline for students in the hospitals: "The greater the trauma, the fewer the words." Or perhaps the story of one of my most memorable student "teachers" could remind us of this most effectively. I shared the wisdom of his answer to an exam question on ministry to persons in grief with readers of *The Journal of Pastoral Care* in an editorial that appeared in the early 1970s. The following are the words shared with me by this rural preacher who had a very limited education:

It is not my policy to ask someone, lest [sic] pray when they have lost their loved one. For this very same person may have prayed more than I have ever prayed. In this case, I would rather be Silence. For I remember when my father die, many people come and say to me, "Brother Rogers, you have my deepest sympathy," but one person come to me without any words of sympathy or quotation of scripture to me. He sat with me. When I would stand up, he stood up. If I walk to the door, he would also walk to the door. I have never been so comforted and warmed by Christian love as I was at that moment. It reminded me of Jesus when Mary came to him weeping and said, Lord if you had been here my brother would not have died. Jesus did not say a word, but groaned in the spirit. Not many people at this time want someone to pray for them but your present and Silence is the best expression for pray at this time.[16]

Another reminder of the limitation of language comes from the experiential, existential side of our psychological tradition. We have been taught in our clinical work to resonate with the affect in a situation—to go after the feeling. Sometimes the stories persons tell enable us to experience their feelings with them; sometimes stories hide feelings. The man who wants the pastor to be sure to get the facts straight is usually one who needs to be helped to get in touch with his feelings about life, to learn the difference between a thought and a feeling. I generally encourage students I am supervising to help people tell their stories and sort out the difference between their thoughts and their feelings.

Pastoral counseling is, most importantly, the offering of relationship—depending upon the skill of the counselor—and using that relationship to help the counselee learn a more satisfying way to deal with all the relationships of life. I have already stated Harry Stack Sullivan's basic postulate that we are all more alike than otherwise—and that means you, me, the schizophrenic patient, the Pharisee, and the publican. Somewhat less familiar is Sullivan's characterization of the human condition as existence on a continuum between anxiety and loneliness. What is most human about us is the pain of life caused by the anxiety of relationship with others—beginning with the mothering one and continuing through life. We avoid anxiety by avoiding relationship, but that avoidance causes the even greater pain of loneliness. So we are pushed back toward relationships and finding a way to deal with the anxiety that they cause. Our ways of dealing with our anxiety, on the one hand, and our loneliness, on the other, express the particular kind of humanness to which the pastoral counselor is called to respond.

The response that is required of us is what I have called, in my book on pastoral counseling, *relational humanness.* [17] I believe that the concept of relational humanness is consistent with the New Testament picture of the Christ in its focus on the interpersonal dimension. At the same time, this concept speaks to the issue of what counseling is to be if it is genuinely pastoral. The norm, relational humanness, is sustained and nourished in the pastor by three ongoing dialogues in which the calling to ministry involves her or him: the dialogue with the Christian story and its meaning for ministry, the dialogue with the role and function of being a minister, and the dialogue with the community which makes and continues one in ministry.

In the book, I mention a long-term counselee who referred to me as a "father, lover, and religious person." I suggested there that this description was not inappropriate for a pastoral counselor. In fact, I continue to explore the meaning of those images as descriptive of what a pastor is. Being and continuing to be a "religious person," whatever that means to the pastoral counselor and to his or her counselee, takes place primarily through the dialogues I have mentioned above. Being a father (or a parent) and a lover involves us in the ongoing challenge of what it is to be in a caring relationship to another human being.

It may be that my use of the term "lover" has so many inappropriate and irrelevant associations that it cannot be claimed for the pastoral relationship. My concern is not so much to make a case for the use of the term as to suggest that some of the discomfort with using it may speak to its importance. I am not at all sure that we can find a completely comfortable term for expressing our human need to give and receive love. As important and exciting as physical loving can be, I am not deeply impressed with my physical abilities as a lover. I am impressed, however, that even I—with all my embarrassment and anxiety—have been able to learn how to offer love to other persons without any physical touch—by offering my presence with very few words to interpret that presence. My impression is that the so-called sexual revolution has allowed many people to become successful lovers sexually but that they have no idea of how to express love without any physical contact. Being loving in a pastoral relationship is to be fully experiential, fully human, fully aware of the other, and yet able to set limits because of responsibility the pastor has for the well-being of the other. I was able to say this with the help of a former client, Joanne. She was able to let me be a "lover" because I was also a parent and a religious person. The limits of what those other terms meant to her allowed the freedom for ours to be a genuinely loving relationship.

I conclude this discussion of the relational language of pastoral counseling with an effort to unpack some of the pastoral meaning of the term *parental* (and its relationship to the *lover* and the *religious person*) through the use of a dream shared with me by a young man who had asked me to supervise his counseling. In seeking to meet the requirements of the American Association of Pastoral Counselors that he have supervision from two different supervisors, he contracted both with me and with a colleague of mine for individual supervision. Rather quickly it became clear that my colleague had become the good guy and I the bad guy. My supervisee perceived my colleague as nurturing, supportive, and understanding of his struggles to learn, whereas he saw me as hostile, judgmental, and certainly not as religious as he had heard I was.

Surprisingly—and believe it or not these things do continue to surprise me—over the months one of us began to change. He perceived the change as taking place in me. I became more caring and understanding, even more religious (although he wished I had let him know that earlier!). Before one of our last sessions together he dreamed this dream. He was going fishing in a lake with which he thought he was familiar. In order to get there he had to go through some woods that seemed strange and unfamiliar. As he was walking somewhat anxiously through the woods, there appeared a large bear which looked at him and then came after him. He ran from the bear and, fortunately, soon came to a small cabin. He ran in and was safe from the bear. In order to remain safe, he had to stay in the cabin, because the bear was roaming around outside. After some time, he decided that he needed help. Even though he was still trapped in the cabin, he was able to go down the road to a country store (how he was able to get to the store without the bear getting him or to be in two places at once is the stuff of which dreams are made!). In the store he asked who he could find to chase the bear away, and to his surprise I appeared and offered to help him. We walked back into the woods together, found the cabin, and chased away the bear.

As you might guess, my supervisee and I had some fun with that one. Among the many things it suggests is the parental quality of the pastoral relationship even when it begins in a simple, contractual way, intended to accomplish a particular, well-defined purpose. It also speaks beautifully of the way a person who becomes aware of needing help can be trapped but go for help at the same time. Theologically, my Methodist heritage would call that prevenient grace. My point here, however, is simply to suggest the power of the pastoral relationship when it is experienced and used. A counselee recently said to me, "You know, I think things began to change for me when I stopped trying to use you to get help with my problems." That might be interpreted as saying, "when I began to trust you and realize the importance of a relationship to someone like you," that is, someone who could be parent, lover, and religious person.

And so we honor our heritage in the pastoral care and counseling movement, celebrating the contributions of persons like Wayne Oates. Like the psychologists and the psychiatrists, we have a new language—this time, one that is our own. It is a new language, but it is also very old, expressing what we have received from our fathers and mothers in the faith. It is *clinical, mediating,* and *relational,* strong as a bear but able to chase the bears away.

6

Pastoral Care with the Aged: The Spiritual Dimension

Albert L. Meiburg

Pastoral concern for the aging has a noteworthy history, rooted in ancient times but being rediscovered today. Within the memory of most of us, this concern has grown and flourished, making its own contribution to the literature of gerontology. Seward Hiltner, while secretary of the Department of Pastoral Services of the Federal Council of Churches, planned the first comprehensive study of the relationship of Protestant churches to older people in 1946. Paul B. Maves, then teaching religious education at Drew Theological Seminary, and J. Lennart Cedarleaf, then serving the Illinois State Training School for Boys, carried out the study and reported it in their classic work, *Older People and the Church.* [1]

The foresight of these pioneers in pastoral care is remarkable. Their study of religion and aging was launched within one year after the formation of the Gerontological Society of America. When their book appeared, the literature on religion and aging could be numbered on the fingers of two hands. In terms of scope, depth, balance, and practical usefulness, *Older People and the Church* still has few equals.

Now, thirty-five years later, where are we in our knowledge of aging and in our practice of pastoral care with older people?

Albert L. Meiburg is Professor of Pastoral Theology, Southeastern Baptist Theological Seminary, Wake Forest, North Carolina.

My effort to answer that question leads me in three directions. (1) Recent decades have seen significant changes in the status of older people and in our knowledge of the aging process. (2) Despite these changes, however, the central issues of aging are essentially spiritual. (3) Pastoral care with older persons needs to be rethought in the light of the current realities of aging, which means addressing the spiritual as well as the other dimensions of aging.

The New Dimensions of Aging:
What's New About Growing Old?

More than a decade ago, when we were culturally preoccupied with future shock, someone remarked that the future was not what it used to be. With some validity, a parallel comment could be made about gerontology. Growing old is not what it used to be either. For example, new developments in the biological and sociological understandings of the aging have implications for the way we conceptualize pastoral care.

In the biological area, various theories of aging are being studied. The molecular, the cellular, the immunological aspects of aging are complex. Why we age is still a biological mystery, but we are reaping returns on studies of aging populations that have extended over many decades. The fact is that the present generation of older people is in better health than any previous one. Over 80 percent of older people are mobile and self-sufficient.

Most early studies of older people looked to institutionalized populations for their subjects. Consequently the studies tended to be "problem-centered." Their findings tended to reinforce the negative social stereotype that equates aging with impairment. This image has been corrected by longitudinal studies, such as those at Duke and in Baltimore, where large numbers of "well" persons have been followed for twenty or more years. To cite one example from the Gerontological Research Center in Baltimore, two groups of individuals were compared, one composed of persons who lived beyond age 75, and the other composed of those who did not. Those who survived beyond 75 had higher levels of kidney function. Such an observation can be made only in a longitudinal study.[2]

New studies of the biological dimensions of aging also result from sophisticated techniques that permit measurement of minute quantities of many important substances, such as enzymes and hormones. When able-bodied healthy males were studied with such techniques, no evidence of any change in the amount of male sex hormone in the blood was found, at least until the age of 75 or 80.[3]

Nathan Shock, for many years director of the Baltimore center, predicts that 70-year-olds in the year 2000 will be healthier and fewer of them will require supportive services.[4] He also notes that we could live longer and do better if we stopped doing the things that kill us and began doing the things we know promote health. I recalled his advice when I happened to notice what was in the grocery cart ahead of me at the supermarket: a pound of lard, a carton of cigarettes, and a six-pack of beer—all the necessities of death!

Recent studies in the biological dimension of aging offer hope that we will not only live longer, on the average, than our ancestors but will be functionally competent to contribute to society and enjoy life while doing so.

The sociological dimensions of aging are also changing. The reduction in the fertility rate combined with increased longevity has resulted in a significant increase in the numbers of older people in our society. During the decade 1965 to 1975, the death rates for those 65 to 74 declined by 16 percent, for those 75 to 84 by 10 percent, and for those over 85 by 25 percent.[5]

In 1870, people over 65 years of age comprised 3 percent of the population. Demographers predict that the proportion of elderly will grow from today's 11 percent to as much as 20 percent by the year 2020. By the year 2000, 44 percent of the old will be over 75.[6] One in 9 persons in the United States is past 65, but in some communities the proportion is closer to one in four. Many church congregations consist almost entirely of people past 50.

We are already experiencing the effects of this population change in terms of its impact on family life. To cite a personal example, I never knew my maternal grandparents, both of whom died years before I was born. This resulted partly from the fact that my mother was one of the younger daughters in a family of twelve children. Today's children increasingly know not only both sets of grandparents but a great-grandparent as well. In fact, as a result of divorce and remarriage, today's children may have six or eight grandparents.

What we have now, according to Bernice Neugarten, is two generations of older people: the "young old" (those 55 to 74) who are relatively healthy and well off, and the "old old" (75 plus).[7] The aging of the family has in many instances added new stress to the lives of some of the young old, who are being called upon to provide care for the very old at a time when they themselves are experiencing some of the "assaults" of aging, such as widowhood, retirement, reduced income, and the onset of chronic illness.

One of the most stubborn social myths of aging concerns family relationships. One basis of this myth is an inaccurate romanticizing of living arrangements in the past, wherein the three-generation household is often held up as an ideal. Historians tell us that this arrangement was not as common as we suppose and that when it did exist it was due to economic necessity rather than personal preference.

A second basis of this myth is the notion that in recent times the ties between the family and their elder members have been severely weakened. According to the "myth of alienation," families rarely see aged relatives. Adult children "dump" their impaired older members into institutions.

Several cross-cultural research studies have refuted this myth. Studies in Scandinavia, Britain, and the United States show that most older people prefer to live close to, but not with, their children. They prefer "intimacy with distance." The same studies show that most older people live within an hour's drive from at least one child and that they have personal contact with at least one child a minimum of once a week. Family members give 80 percent of the medically related and personal care to the chronically limited elderly, and one third of these recipients need constant care.[8]

Another closely related myth is that the providing of community services replaces family care and discourages family caregiving. This idea, too, has been shown to be untrue. A recent study by the New York Community Service Society showed that community services encourage family care, reduce family strain, and enhance the quality of family care.

Thus far, we have noted briefly some of the new biological and sociological perspectives on aging that have a bearing on a "dead end." Psychologists had apparently forgotten the example of the pioneer G. Stanley Hall, who about the turn of the century not only did a classic study called *Adolescence* but followed that with an equally thoughtful work entitled *Senescence*.

Over the past two decades we have deepened our grasp of the developmental tasks facing us in late life. We no longer accept as adequate the concept of late life as an inevitable period of stagnation and decline. As pastors, we are better equipped to challenge older people to discover their potential for change and growth. What are some of these key developmental issues?

Robert C. Peck's essay "Psychological Developments in the Second Half of Life" illustrates how developmental tasks confront the individual with essentially spiritual issues.[9] Peck feels that Erikson's eighth stage (ego integrity vs. despair) is a useful construct and a dominant theme for late life but that it is too general to be helpful when we are looking at a chronological period of up to one third of the life span. Peck envisions three tasks for old age organized around the issues of work and retirement, loss of health, and ultimate meaning.

Ego Differentiation vs. Work Role Preoccupation

Chronologically, this issue begins to be addressed as persons face the end of their children's dependency. Parenting was never intended to be a lifelong vocation. Similarly, retirement requires individuals to define themselves otherwise than by their traditional work roles. This transition raises again the issue of identity —an issue that the person of faith can resolve through accepting the grace of God, who loved us simply for who we are and who we are intended to become—not for what we can *do*.

Body Transcendence vs. Body Preoccupation

In the course of normal aging, all of us will face some sort of physical limits. The spiritual issue here is whether we will allow the physical changes that are a part of normal aging to dominate our lives or whether we can still find challenge and satisfaction in creative mental activities and human relationships. On the one hand, we are tempted to deny the reality of our limits by re-fusing to accept our mortality and creatureliness. On the other hand, we are tempted to plead our limits as an excuse to avoid our responsibility for lifelong stewardship of all our facul-ties.

Ego Transcendence vs. Ego Preoccupation

It is only one step from experiencing the limits of chronic illness to anticipating the ultimate limit of life represented by death. The spiritual choice, as Peck sees it, is between passive resignation, on the one hand, and a deep active effort to make life better for others, on the other.

The spirituality of aging is not a mystical gift that arrives along with a Medicare card on one's sixty-fifth birthday. Certainly not all senior adults take an explicitly religious view of life. Aging, however, does bring with it the *potential* of spiritual growth. Whether or not this growth dimension of aging is nurtured and actualized depends in part on the quality of pastoral care. The aim of pastoral care is to challenge senior adults to discover their unique growth possibilities and to sustain and encourage them to use the resources of their faith.

In the light of both the "new" dimensions of aging—the deep-ened understanding of the biological and social realities of later life—and the abiding spiritual issues which will face all of us who survive to old age, how can we assure that pastoral care is ad-dressing the mainstream concerns of the aging? That is the bur-den of my final point.

Addressing Pastoral Care to the Spiritual Issues of Older Persons

Let us begin with the recognition of the individuality of older persons. Older persons are just as complex and diverse in their development as are children and youth. Every seminarian who has ever served as youth minister knows that twelve-year-olds don't mix very well with high school seniors—and that is only a six-year time span. Therefore, let me suggest three themes for pastoral care with older persons. These themes can be oriented roughly to the levels of need among the aging.

Growth and Directionality

The first theme is that of growth and directionality, appropriate to the needs of the first generation of the elderly, the so-called young old. Significant transitions are likely to occur during the late fifties, sixties, and into the seventies which challenge one's self-concept and require a new sense of direction. The most common of these transitions are the departure of the last child, retirement, relocation, and the death of a spouse. In each case the individuals must redirect their lives in new patterns. Pastoral care can support this process.

The so-called "empty nest" syndrome is probably less traumatic for most parents than the myth would suggest, but there are always those for whom the departure of the last child is tough. Likewise, even when retirement is welcomed, there may be some unanticipated complications. The pastor should not underestimate the significance of this change of status. Well-intentioned friends, and even retirees themselves, may fail to appreciate the impact of the changes that retirement brings.

"Retirement shock" can result from the sense of loss in persons who have strong ties to their work and who find in it a sense of meaning and identity. Harried middle-aged or younger friends, whose image of retirement is that of an unending vacation, are likely to envy their retired friend's independence from schedules and deadlines. They sometimes overlook the possibility that the retiree feels both freedom and loss as a result of retirement. They may joke with the person about all the free time but overlook possible feelings of loss of status and resulting anger.

In *The Desert Blooms,* Sarah-Patton Boyle tells of her own struggle with relocation and retirement.[10] She had enjoyed homemaking, but after her husband left and her children were grown, she decided to move from a college town to the suburbs of Washington, D.C., to begin a new life.

At first, she was busy decorating her apartment to her own taste and exploring the shopping centers, art galleries, parks, and churches. Within a few months, however, she made a painful discovery. Her sense of being free to do *what* she wanted, *when* she wanted, faded. Her desire to paint and write seemed to dry up. The demands of outside pressures from which she had previously escaped through her writing were no longer there. She felt immobilized.

It was natural for Patty Boyle to turn to her church in this crisis. She had been a lifelong Christian. She did, in fact, find friends in the church fellowship, including the pastor and his wife. But despite the helpfulness of many in the church, she found that even there the pain of her personal struggle was only dimly perceived. Her experience shows clearly that we cannot assume that retirement is pure joy. There may be joys in it, but there is also hard work. Patty Boyle learned through pain and struggle that she needed a new "repertoire." She needed to discover a new purpose and direction for her life.

Thus, in caring with the young old we try not to "take care of" or "take over," but rather to assist in the processes of redirection. Challenging the young old to grow socially, mentally, and spiritually—to discover the excitement of caring for themselves, their world, and other persons—will forestall stagnation, loneliness, and self-pity.

Meaning and Identity

A second theme in caring with the elderly is that of meaning and identity, appropriate to the middle phases of aging. William Clements, writing in a 1979 issue of *The Journal of Religion and Health,* suggests that our sense of *"life time"* is the medium within which we face the issues of identity and growth.[11] Whereas in youth there is a sense of limitless time, by middle age focus seems to be on time remaining. But what about late life?

Within the past two decades, we have gained a fresh appreciation of the behavior known as "reminiscing," a phenomenon quite evident here on the occasion of a festival such as that which honors Wayne Oates. Indeed, in Oates's *Struggle to Be Free* we have a beautiful example of the benefits that can result from a review of one's life. Life review is a process of sifting out the kernels of one's own truth and then in grace allowing the wind gently to blow the chaff away.

A distinctive aspect of Wayne's disciplined presentation of his story is that he offers it for a socially redemptive purpose, namely, to stimulate others to reflect on the meaning of their lives. We are not surprised to learn that his readers are writing him to share their stories, a purpose that he hoped to achieve.

Pastoral care in *early old age* may well be given by fostering the process of life review. This review may be a person's most precious opportunity to come to grips with what life has meant. This review may be done in various ways. One does not need to produce a document, but one can be helped by an interested listener, perhaps the pastor.

As we move farther down the time line into *later old age,* Clements notes, a unique shift occurs in the sense of life time. Those who achieve maturity in this phase of life find little satisfaction in the distant future—for they know that in terms of *chronos* time there is little—nor in the distant past. Rather, they find their satisfaction and fulfillment in the eternal *now,* in the living present, in the "lived moment," as Ross Snyder so beautifully puts it.

Sarah-Patton Boyle, to whom I referred earlier, tells how the words of a man confined to a wheelchair following a plane crash awakened a shift in her own time sense. Sam told how he became a prisoner not only of his wheelchair but of time. He was so caught up in mourning the past and dreading the future that he was missing the exciting things that were happening in the present.

In Sam's words, Sarah heard a word of the Lord: "Remember not . . . the things of old. Behold, I am doing a new thing" (Isa. 43:18–19). Focusing on the present helped to lead her out of her bondage to the past and her fear of the future. As she put it, "Good memories can be refreshing, and bad ones can be learned from. But good or bad, when memories hamper present functioning, it is time to turn them out."[12]

When we confront people who are oppressed by their fears of the future or burdened by the memories of the past, we may help them by emphasizing the growth opportunities that lie in the immediate present. The present is the only place life can really be lived, and when we live with full awareness, in the present, we live not just in time but in the context of eternity.

Suffering and Service

A third theme of pastoral care with the aged is that of suffering and service, a theme that addresses both the darker and the brighter side of aging. In the past our picture of aging has been far too gloomy. We now can see that for most older persons late life can become a time of growth and redirection, with new possibilities arising from experience, maturity, and openness. We are aware, however, that older persons also face suffering of one kind or another. There is pain. There is illness. To be effective pastors we must understand in some depth the kinds of pain that are common to older persons.

In old age, as at other life stages, to be ill is to be deviant. The problem is that we, as a society, can tolerate acute illness fairly well, but we have difficulty with chronic pain and illness. Most of the elderly realize this lack of tolerance and tend to minimize their pain. They try not to dramatize their disabilities. Sadly, the result is that those who experience the most pain for the longest time must also experience the greatest social isolation. They often assume that no one is interested in their "story."

As a college sophomore, I was deeply touched by reading Thornton Wilder's *Our Town,* which was not long off Broadway at the time. But there is one passage where I have wanted to argue with Wilder. You remember the point where the Stage Manager, the narrator, says, in effect, this is the way life goes on, one generation after another. People are born, they grow up, they marry, they have children, and they die. Once in a great while, that story is interesting.

That is where I differ with Wilder. It is true that there is a degree of sameness about the "human comedy," but I disagree that the story is not interesting. I find that every person's story is interesting.

As pastors, we care for some persons who struggle with impairments that they will carry the rest of their days. What is our theme then? I remember with poignancy a little lady who for all five years that I knew her was crippled, misshapened, and in pain from arthritis. Her legs were badly drawn, and impossible to straighten. She was bedfast. Despite her limitations, however, she ran a small gift shop from her bed. I never knew her to complain. Her courage, patience, and endurance inspired everyone who knew her.

It was only after she died that I caught a glimpse of the depth of her suffering. Her pastor confided in me that just before she died, she asked him to see if in preparing her body the undertaker could please try to straighten her poor crippled legs. Here was a dear soul, tortured on the rack of a crippling disease, who never complained, yet longed for a restoration of her true self.

Throughout a long confinement, she found a purpose in helping the institution that sheltered her and converted her pain into a genuine participation in the lives of others. Is that not the meaning of this third theme of pastoral care with the aged—*suffering wed to service?* Is this combination not at the heart of our gospel faith? Somehow in the goodness of a merciful God, one whose own Son hung on a cross for our salvation, there is a stewardship even of pain and a service even of suffering.

The frontiers of aging will be pushed back even farther in the days ahead. We will discover new ways to extend life and to make it enjoyable and meaningful. But even if the life span were to be extended to the patriarchal record of hundreds of years, we would only succeed in prolonging for a brief moment our mortality. The enduring issues of aging are not primarily biological, but spiritual. They will not be resolved, in the long run, by science, as helpful as science can be. The only pastoral care with the aging worthy of the name is that which addresses these deep spiritual issues of *growth and directionality, meaning and identity, suffering and service.*

Rabbi Abraham J. Heschel, in his address to the White House Conference on Aging in 1961, put the essence of what I have been trying to say far more eloquently:

> Old people need a vision, not only recreation.
> Old people need a dream, not only a memory.
> It takes three things to attain a sense of significant being.
>> God
>> A Soul
>> A Moment
> The three are always here.
> Just to be is a blessing, just to live is holy.[13]

7

Revisioning the Future of Spirit-centered Pastoral Care and Counseling

Howard J. Clinebell, Jr.

Revisioning, the process of critiquing and revising our guiding images to keep them relevant and responsive to the radical changes emerging in our society, is an essential and continuing task for the field of pastoral care and counseling. The author of Proverbs stated the issue well: "Where there is no vision, the people perish" (29:18, KJV). For us in the caring and healing disciplines, the social irrelevance of obsolete guiding images produces professional frustration and impotence. There is an urgent need for empowering visions that can both guide and energize us as agents of creative change. As John Naisbitt, author of *Megatrends,* puts the issue, "Strategic planning is worthless— unless there is first a strategic vision."[1] In a society of mind-boggling changes, we need an evolving vision that changes as the new age unfolds.

Revisioning should be a collaborative process in which pastoral counselors and counseling pastors from a wide spectrum of theological, clinical, ethnic, and cultural backgrounds interact with each other's insights. By sharing our fragments of insight, we can challenge, stimulate, and enrich each other's envisioning.

Three books have challenged and stretched my thinking about the future: Alvin Toffler's *The Third Wave* (1980), Daniel Yan-

Howard J. Clinebell, Jr., is Professor of Pastoral Psychology and Counseling, School of Theology, Claremont, California.

kelovich's *New Rules: Searching for Self-fulfillment in a World Turned Upside Down* (1981), and John Naisbitt's *Megatrends* (1982).[2] The perspectives of these authors are in the background of my thinking about the future of our field.

The Acceleration of Social Change

A guiding vision for Spirit-centered pastoral care and counseling must be geared to the fact that the speed of social change and social mobility will continue to accelerate through the 1980s and 1990s. The massive changes and uprootedness since World War II will increase in the next fifteen years, as will the resulting personal and family problems. The epidemic of loneliness resulting from the loss of a caring community by millions of people will make skilled pastoral care and counseling increasingly needed.

Alvin Toffler considers that we are witnessing the dawning of a new civilization. He sees the changes to be the single most explosive fact of our lifetime. As he understands human history, there have been three great tidal waves of radical transformation, each inconceivable during the previous wave. The first was the development of agriculture beginning some ten thousand years ago. The second was the beginning of the industrial age some three hundred years ago. This industrial wave created the world in which we have learned to do ministry—the society of nuclear families, sex-role differentiation, bigger cities, larger hierarchical organizations, mass (factory-like) education, centralization, standardization, and synchronization.

The third wave, according to Toffler, began in the mid-1950s, when for the first time white-collar and service personnel outnumbered blue-collar workers, and the computer revolution began in earnest. Humankind faces "a quantum leap forward, . . . the deepest social upheaval and creative restructuring of all time."[3] The long-term promise of this new wave is the development of the first truly human society in history. The short-term reality, which many are already experiencing, is the challenging and shattering of old values and old hierarchical authority relationships; the paralysis of old political systems (such as nation-states); the tearing apart of families (as new family styles are created); and the threatening of the power-privilege positions of white-male-dominated elites (who will produce further chaos by their resistance to the new age). I find that Daniel Yankelovich's image illuminates our situation. He holds that the "continental plates" supporting our culture are shifting dramatically, producing social earthquakes and volcanic eruptions, comparable to what happens when the giant geological plates under the continents shift dramatically.

The third wave will impact pastoral care and counseling profoundly and increase the need for this ministry. A well-known 1957 study sought to discover how many Americans had gone for professional help with personal problems and to whom. It produced what is probably the most-cited statistic in pastoral care literature: viz., one out of seven Americans had gone for such help and 42 percent of these sought help from a clergyperson.[4] A later study revealed that one out of four Americans had sought professional help with a personal problem, and that 39 percent of these had chosen a clergyperson for help.[5] One out of ten Americans said that, at one time or another, they had talked with a minister, a priest, or a rabbi about a personal problem. These facts are particularly impressive when seen in the light of the proliferation of a nationwide network of community mental health centers during the years between the two studies. There can be no doubt regarding the crucial and continuing role of clergy and congregations in providing care and counseling.

The Acute Spiritual-Ethical Crisis

A guiding vision for Spirit-centered pastoral care and counseling must enable us to respond to the acute, escalating spiritual-ethical crisis in Western cultures. This crisis stems at least in part from the changes brought by the third wave. What is the nature of this crisis? There is an epidemic of existential emptiness, ethical confusion, meaning vacuums, spiritual poverty, and pathology, which breeds all manner of personal, relational, and psychophysiological problems. This general spiritual malaise impacts every person who seeks care and counseling. Equally important, for our purposes, it is also a part of our experience as counselors. In our thing-worshiping technological society, transcendence as an energizing belief and experience has largely disappeared from the worldview of millions. Traditional systems of value, meaning, and belief have disintegrated, leaving many in a flat, two-dimensional secularized world. Traditional religious symbols, images, rituals, and institutional forms no longer satisfy them. The bumper sticker I saw not long ago, HONK IF YOU BELIEVE IN ANYTHING, carries overtones of wistful nostalgia for an age when viable beliefs were readily available. Reaction formations to this anxious tie of spiritual transition are everywhere in our society, as spiritually impoverished people "escape from freedom" (Erich Fromm) into simplistic, authoritarian solutions proclaimed by messianic leaders who know how to exploit the spiritual anxieties of our era and use the electronic marvel of television to amass followers and fortunes.

From the perspective of a holistic understanding of ministry, our spiritual crisis presents an unprecedented opportunity to grow up spiritually, to "put away childish things"—the magical, manipulative, ethnocentric, sickness-generating religion that is epidemic in our times. To respond to this challenge, the pastoral care and counseling movement must deepen its theological roots, enhance its spiritual growth methodologies, and develop its unique theological contributions to the healing arts. Our self-identity must increasingly be derived from grounding all that we do in our rich religious heritage and in the continuing creation of caring communities of faith.

A critical dimension of our culture's spiritual crisis is its widespread value emptiness and ethical confusion. In our Baskin-Robbins society,[6] moral decision-making is vastly more complicated and social guidelines more diffuse and conflicted than in other eras of history. In pastoral counseling, value and meaning issues are at the roots of many, if not most, of the agonizing symptoms that motivate people to come for help. Pastoral counselors need to develop more expertise in moral guidance and in nurturing the growth of mature consciences.

The essence of our uniqueness as pastoral counselors—our theological and ethical training—will become increasingly valued in the new world that is emerging. We must recover and update our neglected traditions of spiritual healing and moral guidance, integrating these with the strong emphasis on insights from the human sciences and methods from secular counseling and psychotherapy. By so doing, we can liberate the creative, untapped power of the *pastoral* in pastoral care and counseling.

The Hi-Tech Revolution

A guiding vision for Spirit-centered pastoral care and counseling must respond to and incorporate the hi-tech, computer, communications revolution in our society. The electronic revolution enables us to communicate information on a massive scale at unprecedented speed. Lifelong learning will be the most fundamental task of the new hi-tech era of communications, just as farming was in the age of agriculture and manufacturing jobs were in the industrial era. The communications era will free more and more people from needless drudgery, to spend more of their time in creative ways (or in trivial or destructive leisure activities).

The home computer explosion is only the tip of the iceberg of the communications revolution. Before the turn of the next century many American homes and churches will have a communications center with a computer, video player, and television cable service giving instant access to an immense quantity of news, information, and educational resources. The enormous potentialities for all dimensions of pastoral care, counseling, and education are only beginning to be developed. What are some elements of an appropriate response by pastoral counselors and counseling pastors to this unprecedented opportunity?

The possibilities are limited only by our imaginations, the costs, and our willingness to risk radical innovations. We are challenged to rethink our traditional approaches to pastoral care and counseling. The current uses by some pastoral counselors of videotapes of counseling sessions in supervision and consultation sessions, and their uses as adjunctive resources in pastoral counseling and therapy, are promising beginnings of what will become increasingly widespread clinical uses of the new electronic hardware. Between-sessions "homework" using instructional videocassettes on issues with which particular counselees are struggling, and asking couples in marriage counseling to videotape at home vignettes of their marital or family interaction, are but two illustrations of the many ways in which electronics will enrich the work of the skilled pastoral counselor.

Teleconferencing and video-teleconferencing are already being experimented with as continuing education methods. The use of various combinations of face-to-face teaching with instructional videocassettes, and with teaching and supervision by means of teleconferences, has exciting possibilities.

The field of pastoral counseling needs persons trained both in clinical skills and in computer competencies, who are thus equipped to develop the software needed. The flourishing of the empirical research (including theory-testing and outcome studies) that the field desperately needs can be facilitated by widespread use of computers and data retrieval. Our field needs a data bank with on-line retrieval incorporating the proliferating literature and research studies in our field. I can envision the day when pastors who get in over their heads in counseling situations will be able to hook into a pastoral counseling data-bank consultation network, or "warmline," by means of a computer-telephone hookup, to get the help they need immediately.

The hi-tech electronics revolution can have either a destructive or a liberating impact on human relationships and consciousness. Studies of television and computer addictions and of the negative impact on some intimate relationships of the burgeoning uses of computers suggest the kinds of problems we may face in the future. Maintaining one's primary relationship eight hours a day with an electronic brain which is totally predictable, devoid of emotions, does what is commanded instantly, thrives on endless repetition without protesting, can make relating to a live human spouse a rude transition.

There are profound implications in all of this for personal and marital wholeness. John Naisbitt makes a convincing case for the view that the more we are inundated by hi-tech gadgets, the greater the need for hi-touch to balance and humanize the impact of the gadgets on our psyches.[7] People who feel increasingly like depersonalized punch cards in a faceless automated society will have special need for the counselor's skills in helping them touch meaningfully, communicate deeply, and respond to each other's heart hungers for intimacy.

As Carl Jung once observed, the mythical and mystical aspects of religion may be our most effective defense against the mass-mindedness of a technological society. The hi-tech revolution enhances the need to stay centered in the spiritual core of our human identity—our "higher Self" (Roberto Assagioli) or soul. Only thus can our marvelous machines become primarily instru-

ments of human liberation (from drudgery, hierarchies, and ignorance) rather than forces that tend to mechanize our consciousness, our identities, and our life-styles. Our religious heritage has much-needed light to shed on the issue behind the *what*
of communication, namely, the *why* of communication.

A More Holistic Worldview

A guiding vision for Spirit-centered pastoral care and counseling needs to be informed by the new holism that is emerging in
many fields and the growing influence of the new physics from
which a more holistic and systemic worldview will eventually
develop. This worldview promises to be more open to and com-
patible with the way many pastoral counselors see the sacred as
integral to the so-called secular. The "faith" of science (and of
our Western society) has been dominated by the central themes
of determinism, materialism, mechanism, and Cartesian mind-
body dualism. It is a worldview drawn from classical Newtonian
physics. In contrast, the two pillars of modern physics—relativity
theory and quantum mechanics—are providing increasing evidence that is incompatible with the old mechanistic, dualistic
worldview. This evidence, like that emerging in the fields of
biofeedback and psychosomatic studies, points to one order to
reality in both mind and matter. Recently David Bohm, a leading
physicist, said that there is something mindlike in all matter and
vice versa.

The emergence of systemic, holistic, ecological ways of understanding reality is an encouraging development. The burgeoning
holistic health movement, for example, operates out of a new
paradigm of wholeness, defining health as "high level wellness"
rather than simply the absence of gross pathology.

The new holism and the passionate search for wholeness[8]
challenge us to more holistic perceptions in all our pastoral ministries. Our guiding images in pastoral counseling must transcend
the old medical model (which focuses mainly on the diagnosis
and treatment of pathology), to make pastoral care and counseling robustly wholeness-oriented (and therefore more pastoral),
in both theory and practice. Holistic pastoral care will focus
actively on enhancing the quality of a person's total wholeness,
including physical wholeness. This emphasis will involve utiliz-

ing insights and methods from the body therapies and integrating these methods with the intrapsychic and interpersonal therapies that have been central in modern pastoral counseling. Holistic pastoral care will include such innovations as teaching some parishioner-clients health-sustaining nutrition, hatha yoga, big-muscle exercise, effective breathing, and relaxation-meditation techniques to reduce chronic stress.

The abundant evidence that life-style, value, spiritual and meaning-of-life issues are often among the crucial causes of various psychological, physiological, and psychosomatic illnesses should lead to a new awareness among health care professionals of the vital role that pastoral counselors can play in healing brokenness and nurturing wellness. Pathogenic religion breeds guilt, fear, helplessness, and hopelessness, which seem to immobilize the self-healing and immune systems of the body, making people vulnerable to many types of illnesses.

The discovery that overcoming body alienation can awaken one's spiritual life is paralleled by the discovery that faith, hope, love, and a sense of transcendent purpose can maximize healing and enable one to handle tremendous stress without developing illness. Accordingly, pastoral counselors with insight and skills to help people grow beyond pathogenic belief and value systems to more salugenic ways of satisfying their basic spiritual needs have unique and invaluable new roles in both prevention and healing.

The understandings from our training in psychology of religion, theology, biblical studies, and depth psychology can make at least three corrective contributions to secular conceptions of health and wholeness. First, a depth awareness of the ubiquitous resistances to wholeness called sin (in us as individuals and in our social systems). As Jung made clear, unless we own our shadow side, we will project it onto others with mutually destructive consequences. Second, the ringing affirmation of our religious heritage that the integrating center of wholeness which impacts all other dimensions is the wholeness of our spiritual lives. Third, the awareness that there can be no such thing as privitized "self-actualization" or wholeness apart from others. The only self-fulfillment that is genuinely whole occurs in covenants of mutual commitment to self, other, and community wholeness.

The robust movement in contemporary psychotherapeutic

theory and practice, including much pastoral counseling, toward healing intervention in interpersonal systems such as families is a part of the trend toward holism in our society. We have only begun to develop the full possibilities of the fact that pastors are the only caring and counseling professionals who have direct entrée into many family systems and to a system of systems called a congregation. Biblical images such as the "body of Christ" remind us that systemic ways of thinking are indigenous to our spiritual heritage.

Liberation of Sexual Identity

A guiding vision for Spirit-centered pastoral care and counseling must incorporate the profound, liberating changes in the basic identity of women (and therefore of men) which are occurring in our society. We are in a time of fundamental transformations in the ways in which women are defining themselves, an era that has been described as "the reluctant but inevitable decline of patriarchy." This era is one in which it has become increasingly clear that the eventual consequences of the continuing dominance of the central patriarchal values—conquest, domination, and "success" defined as power over others—are the irreversible pollution of the biosphere and nuclear holocaust.

There is real hope for the planet in the new identities of women—as full human beings in their own right, who must be free to be fully involved in the public as well as the domestic spheres. This revolution in human identity is one of the major turning points in the human story, a revolution that may help the planet survive and one that will eventually impact every area of human life in shaking but salutary ways. As women increasingly redefine and liberate themselves, we men will be confronted more and more by our own need for redefining our identity and for liberation from the wholeness-constricting shackles of male socialization. Those of us who are committing our major energies to ministries of healing and wholeness have a special stake in being open to the threatening but transforming insights of the feminist vision. We must explore some of the implications for pastoral counseling of the feminist vision.

First, we must recognize that the personal is always political, that issues of a woman's personal healing and liberation are inextricably intertwined with the oppressive structures and systems in the institutions of her community and culture. It means that the goal of liberating counseling for women (and for men) must be *empowerment* for challenging and changing the sick institutions, not adjusting to them. All counseling, pastoral care, and education that is truly liberating and empowering must include consciousness-raising, the process of helping women (and men) become aware of the societal forces that are among the causes of their individual problems in living. This awareness leads to the recognition that there are no personal or psychological cures for institutional, systemic illnesses. The only cures are in political action, meaning the use of collective power to change institutions and social structures.

Second, the goal of counseling both men and women must be redefined as wholeness, defined in androgynous terms to emphasize the full development in each sex of both the so-called "masculine" capacities of all human beings—rationality, assertiveness, leadership, etc.—and the so-called "feminine" potentialities of nurture, concern about relationships, and feelings.

Third, the awareness that the so-called "objective" studies of human development and psychotherapeutic theory (as well as other psychosocial sciences) are infected with a deep, largely unrecognized male bias, has shaking implications for how we understand and do counseling and pastoral care with women through the life cycle. The recent work of Carol Gilligan, *In a Different Voice,*[9] reveals the male biases contained in classical studies of moral development by Lawrence Kohlberg and by Jean Piaget. The book by Gilligan and the book *Toward a New Psychology of Women,*[10] by feminist therapist Jean Baker Miller, are "must" reading for those in pastoral care.

Fourth, in developing more effective ways of facilitating spiritual growth and healing of spiritual pathology, we need the insights and images of the feminist theologians to correct and complement the male-oriented theology in which most pastoral counselors and counseling pastors have been trained. We need to listen to the theological challenges of Mary Daly, Rosemary Ruether, and other feminist theologians, as we seek to develop a whole theology of pastoral care—whole in reflecting the riches of the spiritual searchings and findings of women as well as men.

Fifth, to be agents of liberation and growth for women, counselors (male and female) must get their own consciousness raised on the issue of sexism. Many women need women counselors who can understand (from the inside) the special experience of women in a sexist culture and who can serve as role models of women who have claimed their inner power and do not need to hide it to protect male egos. There is a pressing need for more women clergy who have special training and expertise in pastoral care and counseling. These women must discover and develop their unique approaches and resources for caring and counseling, so these may be incorporated into the teaching, and professional identity formation, of pastoral counselors of both sexes.

Changes in Marriage and Family

A guiding vision for Spirit-centered pastoral care and counseling must take into account the profound changes in marriage and family life in our society. Marriage and family, as an institution, is being challenged and changed today as never before in human history. In the last century, the divorce rate in America has increased fifteen times. It doubled in one decade, between 1968 and 1978. Family desertion by both wives and husbands, spouse battering, child abuse, youth delinquency and suicide, and general marital chaos are at epidemic levels in our society.

The increasing pluralism of life-styles and the proliferation of different types of committed relationships have necessitated a redefinition of the meaning of "family." The traditional second wave family with two parents (the wife of whom stays home and practices mothering, wife-ing, and homemaking full time) now represents only a fraction of American families. One in every six families no longer has both a husband and a wife. Nearly half of American families have no children under eighteen. More than one out of four marriages involves a spouse who has been married before. Divorce, remarriage, and blended families are major American life-styles. More than a million couples live together unmarried in more or less committed relationships. I have explored elsewhere some of the profound implications for pastoral care and counseling of these radical changes in family life.[11]

The Need for Both Individual and Social Healing

A guiding vision for Spirit-centered pastoral care and counseling must bring together the personal and prophetic dimensions of ministry, recognizing the radical interdependence of individual healing and growth, on the one hand, and social healing and transformation, on the other. Behind every personal problem is a cluster of societal problems. We must develop ways of doing pastoral care *to* and *through* institutions, to help them become self-renewing social systems in which individual wholeness will be nurtured, not negated. Unless we incorporate our prophetic vision and awareness more effectively in our practice of pastoral care, we will be unwitting chaplains to the injustices in our institutions and social systems.

Three things may help us respond to this challenge effectively. First, we must rethink the interdependence of love and power, both theologically and therapeutically, and make empowerment, not adjustment, the central goal of all pastoral care and counseling. Second, we must use the major themes of liberation theology as key conceptual resources in our field. For persons who are economically exploited or oppressed by the social malignancies of racism, sexism, ageism, classism, militarism, or tribal nationalism, privatized pastoral care and counseling are like therapeutic tranquilizers. The recovery of sight by the blind must not be separated from release of the captives and enabling the broken victims of social injustice to go free. Such can be done by empowering persons through care and counseling as well as training them to work with others to change the systems that cause their brokenness. Third, holistic, socially responsible pastoral care and counseling need to incorporate the perspectives and methods of the radical therapies, including consciousness-raising, in our work and become more countercultural than in the past. Helping people become aware of the role of societal oppression in their personal problems often is the first step toward their liberation.

The Threat of Nuclear Genocide

A viable guiding image for Spirit-centered pastoral care and counseling must be responsive to the most crucial and urgent ethical issue of our times, the awesome threat of planetary nuclear genocide. History turned a decisive corner at 8:15 A.M. on August 6, 1945, when our country dropped the first A-bomb on Hiroshima. Nearly 100,000 people died from the blast and radiation of that relatively small nuclear weapon. I remember the shaking confrontation of visiting the peace park in Hiroshima a few years ago—of seeing the tangled wreckage of reinforced steel which is all that remains of the concrete building at ground zero of that blast. I remember the slab of stone in the museum there with all that remained of a person—the silhouette etched in the stone by the blast.

The two superpowers now possess weapons of death eighty times as powerful as the Hiroshima bomb. They have a total destructive capacity equal to one million Hiroshimas. The scientists now predict that, if either side explodes even a small fraction of its present nuclear arsenal, the resultant pall of smoke and dust in the atmosphere probably will shut out so much warmth from the sun that a "nuclear winter" will result. Viable human history will end, as the biosphere (including the gene pool of humankind and all other species) is irreparably damaged. A major nuclear exchange will destroy all the treasures of the human heritage. In short, our guiding vision of the future must face the real possibility that unless humankind grows up ethically, spiritually, and politically, there will be no viable future. Unless humankind solves this issue, there will be no opportunity to solve any other issue—ever.

Even if we somehow avoid thermonuclear incineration, there is something ethically obscene about humankind spending $40 million an hour ($600 billion a year) and investing half the world's marvelous scientific brainpower in producing increasingly destructive weapons of global suicide. As someone has pointed out, the bombs are already falling on the poor—in our nation and on our poor sisters and brothers (who constitute the majority of the world's population) in all the poor nations of the planet. To let 40,000 children die each day from malnutrition and treatable or preventable diseases, while the arms race roars on toward genocide, is ethically psychotic, a monstrous *sin.* While the arms race impels us to the brink of annihilation, most of us go about our daily lives as if it were not so.

Every responsible, caring human being is called by God to use the ounces of his or her influence, intelligence, and creativity to help avoid foreclosing history. As pastoral counselors, each of us is called to give highest priority to helping prevent, by positive peacemaking, a global Jonestown. This era is the era of the Seventh Beatitude for the planet and certainly for pastoral counselors.

What are some of the things we can do? We can make holistic peacemaking an integral part of all that we do, in ways such as the following. First, we can use our theological and psychological training and research skills to increase understanding of the spiritual, ethical, and psychological causes of the nuclear insanity in the thinking of our society (and all of us). Some of the probably psychospiritual factors that need to be explored are the following: the paranoid projection onto the current "enemy" nation of our own disowned "shadow" side (Jung); our distorted values which allow us to tolerate the ecological obscenity of the arms race; our tribal idolatries which enable us to trust in violence as a solution to conflict between groups, and make our nation, rather than the human family, our ultimate commitment; our psychic numbing, massive denial, anticipatory grief, futurelessness, and despair; and our inner deadness spiritually that makes our love of life and the planet so pale and anemic.

Second, we must work "like a miner under a landslide" (Luccock) to apply our psychotheological insights and our therapeutic skills to help heal our society's collective and ethical and spiritual madness. This work includes helping those with whom we minister become aware of the nature of the nuclear crisis and the chronic impact on our psyches of the ominous "fate of the earth" that threatens us.[12] Helping each other to lift our feelings to a conscious level and to think the unthinkable, then helping each other experience and express them so that we can transcend them, are crucial steps away from denial and toward empowerment for peace action.

The most effective methodology for helping ourselves and others do so is the despair and empowerment process developed by Joanna Rogers Macy and her associates.[13] Everything we know as pastoral counselors about facilitating grief work can be applied to helping people do their "despair work." With our knowledge of group dynamics and counseling, we can lead peacemaking groups committed both to helping each other work through our action-blocking feelings and doing peace action in all arenas, including political action.

Third, we must continue to see the nuclear dilemma in its appropriate theological context and use spiritual resources fully in approaching peace work. The bottom-line causes and cures of nuclear insanity (nuclearism) are theological. Only by keeping our peacemaking grounded in our theological understanding of life and death can we maintain that reality-based hope which people must have to think deeply about our situation and respond with constructive action. We must use our spiritual-theological resources to help people generate images of a transformed future, and also generate a deepening love for our fragile planet and all its creatures. The *push* of terror will never be enough to motivate sustained construction action for transforming the planet spiritually. Only the *pull* of a vision of the new age of empowered shalom, of justice-based peace flowing from a profound love of life, will be effective.

The Need for Transcultural Perspective

A viable guiding image for Spirit-centered pastoral care and counseling must transcend the movement's predominant North American and European middle-class male origins and orientation to become increasingly transcultural and global in its perspectives. The communications network of our planetary global village, jet travel, and the massive migration of peoples among nations will make cross-cultural counseling sensitivities and skills increasingly essential in the years ahead. An encouraging trend evident at the last two meetings of the International Congress of Pastoral Care and Counseling (Edinburgh, 1979, and San Francisco, 1983) was the vigorous participation of a growing number of persons from non-Western and developing countries. It was clear that many of these persons have a new appreciation of the rich indigenous resources for caring in their own cultures. If our movement is to transcend its cultural origins, we Westerners must do a better job of listening to and learning from pastoral counselors from other ethnic, class, and cultural backgrounds, as well as from feminist pastoral counselors.

It is important to remember that a great deal of cross-cultural counseling occurs very close to home. In fact, much of the counseling done in urban settings has some attributes of cross-cultural counseling. For example, with my particular background, I am engaging in cross-cultural counseling, to some degree, whenever I counsel with a woman, a person from another ethnic background, a blue-collar worker, or a person from an affluent background.

What are some characteristics of effective multicultural pastoral counselors? Such persons are aware of their own inevitable ethnocentrism; secure enough in their own personal identity not to need to depend too heavily on their cultural identity; able to celebrate differentness as potentially mutually enriching; open to learn from persons of other cultures, classes, and gender background; aware that all counseling theories and approaches are products of, and therefore limited by, their cultural contexts; firmly rooted in their own particular culture and group, but ultimately committed to the human family with all its diversity.

Carers and counselors whose spiritual identity is rooted in the Judeo-Christian heritage can find rich resources in that heritage for moving toward a more transcultural, inclusive identity, in which their citizenship in the human family and the biosphere is their ultimate center of loyalty and caring. Such a relatively (it is never more than partial, of course) detribalized, inclusive identity can enable one's caring and counseling to contribute in small but significant ways to the emerging global conscience, caring, and community upon which planetary wholeness and peace ultimately depend.

Developing Right-Brain Approaches to Healing

A viable guiding image for Spirit-centered pastoral care and counseling must encourage us to develop more right-brain approaches to healing, learning, and growth, and to balance and integrate these with left-brain approaches. For many people (including many pastoral counselors) in our scientific, technological, mathematical, verbal culture, healing and wholeness require their discovering and developing their neglected right-brain resources. We need to use many more nonanalytic, intuitive, metaphoric, imaging, storytelling, playful methods of pastoral care and counseling than in the past. These right-brain methods will complement and help to balance the valuable left-brain analytical, rational, lineal methods that have dominated our field in its modern period. It is noteworthy that some of the most skilled therapists—Fritz Perls and Milton Erikson, for example—have been those who were in touch with and able to integrate their right-brain therapeutic capacities with their left-brain capacities.

This movement toward more "whole brain" healing methods should be a natural for pastoral counselors and counseling pastors. For we have the rich, largely untapped right-brain resources of a spiritual heritage full of archetypal images, stories, rituals, myths, and metaphors which have tremendous potential for use in healing and growth work. In spiritually transforming religion, right-brain creeds, theologies, and ethical codes are balanced with right-brain religious experience, life commitment, and gut-level and heart-level beliefs. Rational, analytical intentionality is balanced by metaphoric, symbolic, playful, worshipful celebrating. The God of justice is balanced by the God (or Goddess) of mercy, forgiveness, and grace.

There are other prominent trends in our society that will not be discussed here because of limitations of space. For instance, longer life expectancy confronts us with unprecedented challenges and opportunities in pastoral care and counseling to enable more and more of us to use the gift of increased longevity as a blessing rather than a burden.

The threat and promise of the new leisure is another rapidly emerging social reality with significant challenges to our field. Already the average nine-to-five working person has over four months of leisure time each year. As computers and automation increase, leisure time will multiply, with four-day work weeks and earlier retirement becoming commonplace. Personal and family problems stemming from uncreative uses of leisure will proliferate in the years ahead. Think of the exciting possibilities we face in helping people learn the deep satisfactions of committing more of their free time to generative activities that have some promise of making the world a little better place for the children of the whole human family.

Finally, I hope that those of us who are interested in revisioning the future of pastoral care and counseling will incorporate in our guiding vision and our work the growing evidence of the healing power of laughter. Norman Cousins's account[14] of his use of humor in self-healing from a major medical problem, on which the medical profession had nearly given up, reminds me of the words of a seventeenth-century physician, Thomas Syden-ham. He put the matter well when he said, "The arrival of one clown has more beneficial influence upon a town than 20 asses laden with drugs." If we laugh more *at* ourselves and *with* each other, we will be healthier ourselves, as well as more effective healers. As Sam Keen makes clear, health-nurturing religion must be danced and not just believed. Perhaps we pastoral counselors need to do more dancing and singing and laughing.

The future calls us, as carers and counselors, to increase and use our knowledge and skills to help the church become what the divine Spirit longs for it to be—a wider, deeper channel through which the springs of justice and love from that Spirit can flow into parched and barren lives, relationships, groups, and institutions. The continuing rebirth of this vital art of ministry depends on the willingness of people like us to dream and to dare, to work and to laugh, to love and to pray, with our sisters and brothers in pastoral care and counseling, in many places around the planet. Then we become co-creators with them of the new age of trans-formed consciousness and caring community, which is God's dream for the human family.

8

The Oates Agenda
for Pastoral Care

Walter C. Jackson III

Pastoral care is an ancient Christian discipline. Its practice was taught and modeled by Jesus in his earthly life and activated by his disciples in the early church. Throughout the Christian centuries, pastoral care has taken many forms, although its characterization as the shepherding activity of Christians in the guiding, healing, sustaining, and reconciling of themselves and their non-Christian neighbors serves as a general description. The twentieth century has experienced a renaissance of Christian pastoral care. Among Protestant Christians, the names of Anton Boisen, Russell Dicks, Carroll Wise, Paul Johnson, Seward Hiltner, and Wayne Oates emerge as early leaders. This chapter has as its purpose to sketch in broad outline the features of the agenda for pastoral care in the writings of Wayne E. Oates.

Biographical Considerations

Wayne E. Oates has been an intellectual leader in the discipline of pastoral care for almost four decades. At this writing, forty-four books and more than two hundred and fifty articles, book chapters, and pamphlets represent his literary contribution to the field. And he continues to deliver articulate and helpful

Walter C. Jackson III is Professor of Ministry, Southern Baptist Theological Seminary, Louisville, Kentucky.

writings for use by a growing fellowship of pastors and ministry specialists engaged in the variety of tasks of pastoral care.

The autobiographical rule predicting that writers will speak from their personal experiences is intensely true of Wayne Oates. Born into and reared in a poverty-bound, single-parent, nuclear family of textile mill laborers in 1917, he began as a very unlikely candidate to become a moving spirit in the pastoral care renaissance of the twentieth century. His struggle to free himself[1] from the South Carolina version of the forces of industrialization which have dehumanized people in so many cultures set the stage for the development of his ministry to persons likewise locked into the "plight of humankind." The factors operating in the process of his liberation from an almost inevitable life of menial labor were his own vow to escape, his diverse personal gifts, and his immense determination. But the most important key to escape was the way in which he was assisted by a variety of persons in many stations of life.

Among those persons were a host of "mother-goodwives" within the poverty culture who nurtured him, especially a Mrs. Ingle, whose prophetic message to him was, "You are not supposed to live your life like the rest of us have had to live ours. God has a purpose for you. You must find it." Her message inspired hope and courage. Oates says of Mrs. Ingle, "I have never forgotten her or what she said. I took it to heart. I believed it."[2]

In a one-of-a-kind event, Wayne Oates was chosen to become a page in the U.S. Senate. He received his high school education and his introduction to life in the middle and upper classes of society in the nation's capital. In addition to his schooling, he was informally educated by a senator's wife, his employment supervisor, and other caring adults in an effort to refine his "bumpkin" ways and teach him proper grammar, etiquette, and deportment. In this way, social and cultural discipline were added to his previously mastered academic and survival disciplines. At sixteen years of age, the mandatory retirement age for a Senate page, Oates returned to South Carolina to complete his high school education and to work as an employee of a federal agency. Upon graduation from high school, he secured a job as a weaver in a textile mill, where he worked for nineteen months. The pain of hard work, boredom, and being exploited created an immense unhappiness. These experiences intensified his vow to secure an education in order to free himself from the poverty culture.

His dream to begin a college education began at Mars Hill Junior College in the fall of 1936. At that time, his primary goal was to become a lawyer-politician. He was a diligent student and entered the political arena by being elected president of the largest and .most prestigious organization for students in that Baptist institution: the Baptist Student Union. At Mars Hill, he was again befriended by persons who nurtured and challenged him to a growing life of productivity. Peers, professors, and ministers entered his world as caring friends and companions.

In the process, the Christian faith had begun to play an increasing role in his personal development. His own basic faith, inherited from his family and culture, included an unshakable belief in God and reverence for the Holy Scriptures. Earlier encounters with Southern evangelical clergy, however, taught him to dislike ministers who treated converts as less than persons. Such ministers stimulated in Wayne the lifelong practice of intentional care for persons as people, especially new Christians, and of developing nurturing and feeding relationships with them rather than extractive and manipulative ones. During his college years he received the sensitive religious instruction he had lacked as a teenager. He discovered God as a presence, a "heavenly father" who was a substitute parent able to fill the aching void created when his human father abandoned his mother and four children shortly after Wayne's birth. He also came to understand the heart of the Christian faith to be a personal encounter-commitment to Jesus Christ; an event-act around which he was to organize his life and his understanding of pastoral ministry.

During his twentieth year, Oates sensed an invitation from God to become a vocational minister. Without seeking public recognition, he privately and quietly accepted God's call with a steadfast inner commitment of his growing gifts for such ministry. He completed his undergraduate work at Wake Forest College, where he became a part-time instructor in humanities. Simultaneously, he became pastor of a small rural Baptist church. Here he developed a collegial relationship with a medical doctor who taught him the value of healthy religion in relationship to one's physical and emotional health. Here he experienced the joy and the difficulties of being a pastor to persons locked in the human situation. And here he met and married Pauline, allowing both of them to develop and experience the loving pleasures of an intact nuclear family for the first time.

Wayne and Pauline moved to Louisville, Kentucky, in 1940, where Wayne began his theological studies at the Southern Baptist Theological Seminary and where he ultimately completed his Th.D. degree. Part of that life-directing experience included clinical pastoral education in a general hospital under Ralph Bonacker and a summer unit of clinical pastoral education at Elgin State Hospital in Illinois under the supervision of Anton Boisen. With encouragement from the theological faculty of Southern Seminary, and in particular from Professor Gaines S. Dobbins and President Ellis A. Fuller, Wayne was invited to develop a modern department of Psychology of Religion and Pastoral Care for the seminary.

Theology

Wayne Oates is best known professionally as a writer and then as teacher, counselor/psychotherapist, supervisor, chaplain, pastor, and preacher. His personal competence in these activities is without question, and his scholarly preparation and clinically refined skills are well documented. Oates's writings are filled with digests and interpretations of scores of contributions from ancient and contemporary writers, scholars, and thinkers of many disciplines. His extensive private practice of counseling, as well as his teaching of graduate theological students in pastoral care and medical students in psychotherapy, is unique in the annals of clergy and physician education. In brief, his credentials as a knowledgeable theologian and behavioral scientist are beyond question.

Christian Presuppositions

One factor alone, however, sets Wayne Oates apart from his peers: his radical commitment to the Christian worldview and the thoroughgoing manner in which he makes use of the Free Church tradition within the Christian family of denominations. The major difference in the teaching of Wayne Oates is not so much a difference in kind from other Christian instructors of pastoral care as much as it is a difference in degree. Five factors demonstrate this degree of difference.

First, Oates is an openly declared revelationist. The Christian worldview is the background, framework, and content of his understanding. God's self-revelation in the Bible; the theological and practical wisdom of the Hebrew-Christian Scriptures; and the biblical view of humanity, history, personality, and the meaning of existence, are the foundational bases for his theoretical and methodological teachings.[3]

Second, Oates is an orthodox trinitarian Christian.[4] It is essential to mention this fact, because in Oates's writings the reader will notice the intensively devotional flavor and confessional descriptions of the individual "persons" and "functions" of God the Father, Christ the Son, and the Holy Spirit. For Oates, the understanding of God as a three-in-one unity is revelationally accepted and reinforced in each person's experience, experience that contextually validates the biblical revelation of the triune nature of God.

> The relationship to God the Father, God the Son, and God the Holy Spirit is no abstraction to us; this relationship is life itself. . . . The transformation of the trinity of experience into a doctrinal party cry is a poor substitute indeed for the encounter which the doctrine seeks to catalyze in one generation after another. Rather, the internal birth and sustenance of selfhood and identity come from the obedience to the command of God the Father, the Son, and the Holy Spirit.[5]

The Christian understanding of the trinitarian nature of God is part of the fabric of the revelation of God reinforced in the day-by-day experiences of each believer. Those aspects which defy logical description or clarifying analogy are accepted by Oates as part of the "mysteries" of the faith.[6]

Third, Oates declares relationships to be the most important value in existence.[7] He is a theistic personalist. For him, the primary value of the Bible is in its exclusive ability to enable a religious seeker to encounter the person of God. The Bible is God's word of invitation to persons to enter a divine–human dialogue; the human response to God is to be found in the practice of prayer. "Prayer is another word for relationship with God."[8] In a more human sense, all dialogue is relationship-producing. Pastoral care in all its varieties and expressions is the disciplined process of relationship-building between persons, the end result of which is to assist the minister and the person cared for to be rightly related to God in whatever circumstance or time frame they discover themselves to be.

Fourth, the teaching of the Christian doctrine of humanity is crucial to the Oates agenda for pastoral care.[9] For him, human beings are created and finite—the potential source of their joy or pain. Humans are bipolar and linked to nature by their physical, mental, and emotional dimensions and linked to the supernatural by their spiritual or religious dimensions. They are hopelessly conflicted and unable to achieve their spiritual destinies—doomed to live lives of separation, meaninglessness, and alienation from God; namely, lives of sin. They possess the power of choice—but while their chief end is to worship God and enjoy him forever, they consciously choose less worthy foci (idols) for worship and service. They are pulled between living "other-directed" (heteronomous) lives and "self-directed" (autonomous) lives, a dilemma best resolved by durable commitment to the trinitarian God acted upon by choosing and living Christ-directed (theonomous) lives.[10]

Finally, God *calls* everyone into a personal, spiritual relationship through Jesus Christ.[11] God is the initiator; the person is the reactor. One can know that an authentic relationship with Christ has been achieved when one has a clear awareness of God's forgiveness and has achieved a new understanding of one's spiritual autobiography. In the process, the believer achieves a new sense of awareness of *"who* Christ is, as to who Christ would have him *to be* and what Christ would have him *to do* with his life."[12] As Christ, God has called everyone into relationship and vocational commitment. In response, the believer is called into a covenant of a developing relationship in which the believer achieves the mind of Christ.[13]

Relationship to Secular Writers

Writers with purely humanistic presuppositions, especially those in the human sciences, have been read eagerly by Wayne Oates. Their contributions are valuable in that they provide new insights for deeper understanding of the biblical witness. In addition, the language and ever-changing images of their own generations are excellent vehicles by which to communicate the eternal truths of the Bible in contemporary ways. On the other hand, their contributions are to be compared diligently with and corrected by the wisdom of the Judeo-Christian tradition. It is tragically true that behavioral scientists so often deal with the deep problems of the human situation without benefit of the data and experience of the Christian community.[14] The important goals of the pastoral care theologian in conversation with non-Christian writers is to supply them with the Christian data and wisdom they lack and to relate to them as pastoral evangelists.[15]

Wayne Oates exemplifies this advice in his own writings. Several writers' images and models are frequently used as vehicles to communicate the "eternal truths." A few examples are offered here, beginning with Sigmund Freud, the person Oates credits with doing "more than any other one person in the last hundred years to secularize the ministry of reconciliation of man with himself and man with his fellows. This ministry was originally the concern of only the Christian minister. Freud staked a claim for science for this territory."[16] Freud's bipolar model of personality focusing the dialogue between conscious and unconscious dimensions is used frequently in "corrected form." Freud's "self-within-a-self" dualism is redrafted as obvious aspects of the holistic personality of the biblical witness. Freud's shorthand definition of mental health as one's ability to love and to work is used as a measure for pastoral counselors to diagnose healthy behavior and as a guide to direct counseling interventions designed to increase the flow of positive affection or creative activity.

Of greatest use, Oates insists, is Freud's listing of the three positive functions of religion: to reduce the idolatrous importance of a person's nuclear family; to provide a sublimating methodology and an ethical mooring for one's potentially destructive sexual impulses; and to lift the person's eyes to the truth of one's participation in and responsibility for the whole family of mankind.[17] For Oates, this contribution by Freud bears unmistakable imprinting from Freud's Hebrew heritage.

In his own thinking, Oates demonstrates a decided preference for the individual psychology of Gordon Allport and its focus upon the uniqueness of each personality's growth and development to maturity. Of additional usefulness is Allport's definition of religion as the process of a mature person becoming identified in a meaningful way with the whole of being.[18] Robert J. Havighurst's contributions to the understanding of human growth in terms of "teachable moments" and "developmental tasks" are used by Oates in the nurture of persons receiving pastoral care as well as growing ministers and physicians. Other writers, such as Erik Erikson, Jean Piaget, Prescott Lecky, and Gardner Murphy, have developed systems useful to pastoral care ministers.

Of special note is Oates's use of the work of Harry Stack Sullivan. His psychiatric attention to the development of personality through interpersonal communication and his valuable insight related to the search of each individual for meaningful community are exceptionally helpful in designing individual and group pastoral care strategies. In *The Psychiatric Interview,* Sullivan urges therapists to care for clients as "people," not as "cases," and provides a four-step process model of an interview, with careful attention to such issues as the "process of detailed inquiry" and "termination."[19] The usefulness of such language and images to a comprehensive approach to pastoral care is easy to see.

In his writings, Wayne Oates has addressed pastoral care practitioners of every specialization. Some specific applications of items within the Oates agenda for pastoral care have been selected as illustrations in what follows.

Pastoral Care Agenda for Pastors

Pastors, as well as students in training to become pastors, are a primary audience for the Oates agenda for pastoral care. His first published book, *The Christian Pastor,* is currently in its third edition. The symbolic role and functional methods of the pastor formed the major content of the first edition, where Oates described the total pastor's task.[20] The second edition shifted the emphasis from a task-oriented and work-centered definition to a being-centered and identity-centered integrity as a basis for understanding the symbolic and functional dimensions of the pastoral office. The third edition's focus on the symbolic power of the pastor presents the pastor as more than a "walking job description." The pastor is God's influential and powerful representative in the relational exercise of the preaching, teaching, and caring ministries. Each edition, is, however, "a practical guide for the average pastor in a specific church as the pastor exercises this ministry of pastoral care."[21]

The Pastor's Crisis Ministry

First, "pastoral care can be defined as the Christian pastor's combined fortification and confrontation of persons as persons in times of both emerging crisis and developmental crisis."[22] This activity on the pastor's part requires skillful attention and precise responses to such events as childbirth, religious conversion, vocational crises, marriage, physical illness, bereavement, and death.[23] Wisdom motivates the pastor to be sufficiently attentive, informed, and disciplined to discover crisis events involving members of his or her parish. Each pastor is aware that every crisis either contributes to the positive growth and maturity of the parishioner or to regression and possible reinforcement of negative or pathological patterns. To stimulate emotional and spiritual growth, energetic and skillful pastoral interventions are necessary.

A pastor can and must prepare for crisis ministry in at least three ways. First, the pastor must pay specific attention both to the major forms of reaction generated by crisis events—anxiety, fear, sadness, guilt, loneliness, abandonment, grief—and to the major character of the anxiety produced by the crisis—economic, finitude, legalistic, or other specifically religious concerns.[24] Second, both the best behaviorally oriented methodologies of response and the rich variety of responses suggested within the Christian tradition are to be faithfully and steadfastly employed. Third, a consistent and durable pastoral relationship with each individual and family having experienced a major crisis trauma is necessary for appropriate pastoral care.

An example of how Oates addresses crisis ministry can be found in his work on the common denominator of human experience—bereavement. His dynamic approach to grief sees grief as a process with identifiable stages such as: (1) shock, (2) numbness, (3) struggle between fantasy and reality, (4) breakthrough of feelings—such as profound sadness, guilt, anger, and relief, (5) selective memory with stabbing pain, and (6) recovery.[25] Sensitivity to stage-appropriate interventions of this grief process includes an awareness of the varieties of grief: (1) anticipatory grief, (2) sudden or traumatic grief, (3) no-end grief, (4) near-miss grief, and (5) delayed grief.[26] Awareness of the available pastoral ritual responses to grief is a pastoral necessity. Further-more, an alert minister will organize and instruct the church family about the many ways in which its members might serve as pastoral care persons providing spiritual meaning to people in the catastrophe of grief.[27]

The Pastor's Symbolic Role, Function, and Power

The role and the function of a minister serving as pastor have been powerfully affected through the centuries of Christian cul-ture and tradition. In that sense, the pastor becomes an image of all that is represented by the office of "pastor." An image is always something that possesses the qualities of reality to such a degree as to bring that reality vividly to mind, and when used as a verb it means to represent that reality.[28] Pastors, then, largely derive their authority from the representative power of their office.

A second and more potent source of pastoral power, however, is to be found in the pastor's own personal experience of the gospel and in the actual exercise of the pastor's own pastoral gifts. Pastors possess the authority of "eyewitnesses of that which they declare to others." Pastoral authority rests "in the full exer-cise of preaching, teaching, and caring ministries."[29]

On the basis of the pastor's broadly based empowerment for ministry, the pastor declares himself or herself to be and to function as a representative of God, to serve as a reminder of Jesus Christ, and to be a follower of the leading of the Holy Spirit. The pastor also serves as a representative of a specific church and is a shepherd of the non-Christian.

As God's representative, the Christian pastor should strive to free persons from bondage to their own self-reflection in the mirrors of their chosen conscious and unconscious idols and bring them into a life-giving loyalty to Christ. Even limited success with such a task introduces the pastor's great temptation: "To confuse the symbolism of the pastoral role with the reality of God." A pastor must cultivate humility and gratitude to God for any occasion of success as God's representative.

As a reminder of Jesus Christ, the pastor is to create and re-create right relationships between parishioners and God and to do this within a "relationship of a trusted motive," having earned by demonstrated faithfulness permission to promote the well-being of those who look to their minister for care. In this way, the pastor becomes an undershepherd like Jesus, who listens to and provides for his "sheep," rather than one who functions as a "pseudosovereign who rules his subjects." The central personal goal of the pastor is to see to it that "Christ be formed" in his or her own personality and to seek that for his or her parishioners. In a manner similar to the psychological concept of "identification," human beings may identify with God by gratefully accepting the transforming love of Christ.[30]

As a follower of the leading of the Holy Spirit, the pastor activates the promises of Jesus about the work of the Spirit. Through the pastor, the Spirit's work is to teach, to create community, to give encouragement, and to challenge each worshiper and inquirer to cease idolatrous life-styles and move toward a life of worship focused on the creator God, who has revealed perfect love and forgiveness through Jesus Christ.[31]

Pastors are also to understand that they "symbolize and represent a *specific congregation of people.*" Every pastor's ministry is largely affected by the tradition and history, as well as the "personal opinions, and even the passing whims of this group of people." The Christian pastor must speak *unto* the congregation but must also speak *for* them in every aspect of ministry. Happy is the pastor and the church whose definitions of ministry for their specific congregation have a high level of congruity.[32]

The pastor symbolizes both the congregation's images and the biblical images of interpreter and evangelist. When non-Christian persons respond to the minister or to the church, however, "the minister is responsible, as a witness to the gospel, for relating himself in some challenging and dynamic way to those persons."[33] Of his own pastoral ministry to non-Christians, Oates said:

> My main reason for visiting them was to get them to come to church. If they had never professed faith in Jesus Christ, my simple appeal was that they accept him as their Savior and be baptized, and I promised to continue to follow their spiritual growth. *If they*

did not do this, then I continued to be interested in them as their friend and pastor. [34]

Oates sees his own experience and teaching as being different from an outspoken minority among Southern Baptists who either restrict their ministry to people who come to the church or visit non-Christians only for the purpose of winning converts. Because the Christian pastor is a representative of the God who created every human person, the pastor is to continue a faithful ministry to the non-Christian as well.

Pastoral Methods

The Oates agenda also gives specific attention to pastoral care methods. The first method is to recognize specific influences that condition a pastor's methods of relating to persons seeking assistance. The first such influence is what Oates calls *the Christian equation.* A pastor responds to Christians and non-Christians in different ways even when their situations are nearly identical, "because the religious attitudes of the persons involved give a different structure to the basic difficulty."[35] A person's *level of initiative* is a second important conditioning influence. Questions such as "To whom else have you been able to talk about this?" or "How is it that you have come to me?" enable the pastor to judge the intensity of the search and assess the quality of the guidance the person has already secured in relation to the matter at hand. A third conditioning influence relates to the parishioner's expectations, and those of the church itself, of the *social role of the pastor* as counselor. Other variable factors—such as availability of an *appropriate time* and *social setting,* the person's *level of intelligence,* the *family situation,* and the *physical and mental health* of the person—not only influence but often dictate the manner in which the pastor's assistance is delivered.

An important method for the pastor is that of making diagnostic generalizations relating to the general symptoms of the physical health of the person seeking help. Knowledge related to asking appropriate questions about the parishioner's basic functions, such as sleeping, eating, working, and communicating, enable the pastor to function as an early warning system of potential illnesses. Awareness of the symptomatology and symptom patterns of mental ill health is also of great usefulness to a pastor. In addition, the pastor needs to cultivate consultive and referral-oriented relationships with a variety of medical and nonmedical specialists in order to make the expertise of those persons easily accessible to the parishioners under the pastor's care.[36]

One of the more useful methods for pastoral operations relates to the pastor's use of the concept of *levels of pastoral care*.[37] This concept is based on the social relationship model of personal interactions and is a major aspect of the Oates method of pastoral operations. To use this method, a pastor gives careful attention to the quality of interpersonal interaction with others and becomes aware of being related to them as stranger, acquaintance, or guest. Even the relationship category of welcomed or invited guest precedes a distinctly pastoral role, because the first level of pastoral care is *the level of friendship*. Oates insists that friendship is "the indispensable necessity for all other deeper level of pastoral work. It is the seed bed of any fruitful source to people."[38] At this level, the ordinary events of life, including joy and celebration, are shared in a common life-together flow of experiences.

The second level of pastoral care is *the level of comfort*, in which the pastor walks into "the valley of the shadow of death" with parishioners in their developmental or traumatic crises. At this level, the pastor will use methods of suggestion, catharsis, reassurance, and support. The pastor, it is hoped, will have tested these procedures and interventions in periods of supervised ministry or through years of reflection upon actual pastoral practice. Only those procedures found to be helpful and appropriate will be used. The religious resources of prayer, meditation, worship, and Scripture are the primary tools for pastoral use in ministry at the level of comfort.

The level of confession introduces a pastoral ministry often neglected by Protestant Christians. Every profession contains what Washington Gladden called "the rankling secret." The load of shame and remorse can be removed if the pastor can hear the secret "and convince the troubled soul, *first by his own forgiveness*, that the Infinite Love is able to save to the uttermost all who trust in him."[39]

The level of teaching is an important level of pastoral care. "Jesus most often appeared to his followers as a teacher." Whatever the pastor's counseling style, some element of didactic discourse is essential. Often, the sensitivity of the pastor to individuals in small groups where he or she has a teaching assignment may encourage church members to move toward the pastor for consultation on a one-to-one basis. The pastor "functions as an instructor of the conscious minds, the moral intentions, and the undisciplined desires of [his] people." Most Christians expect their pastor "to be an interpreter of the mind of Christ, . . . an authority on the teachings of the Bible and Christian history."[40] Church members also expect their pastor to be "a repository of information" on a variety of subjects and especially "on the common ventures of everyday life." The pastor must function as a teacher.[41]

The next level is *the level of brief pastoral dialogue,* or short-term pastoral counseling. In such a situation, the pastor assesses the parishioner's ability to respond with comfort to a brief personal dialogue that includes the following: (1) The pastor listens to the parishioner and enables the parishioner to speak freely, (2) the pastor gives a factual summary to verify having heard accurately what the parishioner has said, (3) the pastor asks the person to help outline alternative plans of action with some prediction of the necessary investments and expected outcomes of each, (4) the pastor then "is to appeal to the basic desire of the person." In the rest of the conversation, the parishioner verbalizes the decision necessary to be made, or perhaps informs the pastor of the decision already made, with gratitude for the pastor's listening ear and support. In most instances, some noticeable degree of additional maturing and responsibility comes to a parishioner so cared for. The pastor has been careful to avoid the hazard of giving specific advice so the door is open for specific conversation related to future needs.[42]

The final level is *the level of pastoral counseling and psychotherapy.* Not every inquirer has a life situation that can be resolved in a brief pastoral dialogue. In such instances, the pastor will be aware that a deeper level of pastoral response is required.

Fortunately, a minister today can receive training in many theological schools, hospitals, clinics, and counseling centers, both to learn theory and techniques and to receive careful supervision in the art of pastoral counseling and pastoral psychotherapy. A twenty-eight-page general overview of a deeper-level series of pastoral counseling interviews is provided in *The Christian Pastor*. The summary is sufficiently instructive to assist pastors in avoiding some major errors in pastoral counseling. The Oates admonition that the minister should never become overconfident of his own skill in the use of any technique of pastoral care is most important to notice.[43]

The Pastor's Ministry of Introduction

Some parishioners require the context of a specialized relationship a pastor may choose not to or be unable to fulfill. Following Boisen, Oates divides these persons into three categories.

First, there are those who are capable of taking care of themselves, and will get along nicely regardless of the care the pastor gives them. . . . Secondly, there are those who will become progressively worse, regardless of the care and attention the pastor can offer them, and will not profit by anything the pastor does for them because they do not want to be helped. . . . Thirdly, there are those that stand at the crossroads, and the outcome of their lives will be *largely determined* by the pastor's patient efforts in ministry to them.[44]

For persons from each group, it will occasionally be the pastor's choice to make a referral for those persons who could profit from specialized attention. It is the pastor's responsibility to establish friendships with professional people in a variety of disciplines so as to make persons of many professional disciplines available to the church members when necessary.

Pastoral Care Agenda for Counselors

The pastor *is* a counselor. Congregations of Christians and the general public hear a pastor's public words, observe the pastor's behavior, and maneuver to have some of their counseling needs met in public meetings or private conversations. Every pastor is a counselor but does have a choice as to whether that counseling will be offered in a disciplined and skilled way or in an undisciplined way.[45]

Caught in such a dilemma, many pastors with little or no previous instruction or supervision in counseling either avoid disciplined efforts to learn or latch on to oversimplified meth-

odologies borrowed from secular disciplines that are not carefully assessed in their relation to the eternal God. So much
other-directed pressure is placed on today's success-motivated
pastors to become all things to all people that they quickly fall
into step behind easy-to-follow counseling bandmasters with little or no effort to judge the counseling systems and techniques
for compatibility with the wisdom of Scripture or the pastor's
own faith tradition.

An even greater tragedy befalls pastors who attempt to secure
professionally competent instruction and supervision at the
hands of pastoral counseling specialists whose own professional
education reflects an "overdependence . . . upon psychoanalytic
presuppositions" without having subjected such presuppositions
to the light of Christian faith. Such education leads pastors "to
fundamental confusion as to the nature of religious experience
and the practice of pastoral counseling."[46]

Definition of Pastoral Counseling

Pastoral counseling is a "spiritual conversation" between a
pastor and a painbearer in which the deeper ramifications and the
larger and longer purposes of the painbearer's life itself are
considered. While it may include the very best skills and techniques available to the counseling professions, it is more than
method. Pastoral counseling is not the

> tinkering in an amateurish fashion with the removal of this or that
> symptom. The pastor believes in God, that he is, and that he is a
> rewarder of them that diligently seek him. He joins upon a search
> with the seeker after life much more than he gives "pat answers" to
> deep life issues, thereby relieving the person of the anxiety of asking
> and seeking.[47]

The goal of pastoral counseling is the "spiritual growth and the
achievement of insight" of the counselee. It "presupposes that
the deepest changes in personality occur when the revelation of
God springs up within the counselee's own internal frame of
reference rather than when it is projected into his consciousness
by another person." The pastor is an encourager, a companion
providing "spiritual fellowship" for the "pilgrimage of
growth."[48] Often, pastoral counseling is a "sweaty participation"

by the pastor with parishioners "in their life-and-death struggle for moral integrity in relation to God."[49] The entire process, while able to be divided into multiple segments, is a

> conversation that takes place either implicitly or explicitly within the commonwealth or eternal life as we know it in Jesus Christ. The way of life we have known in times past, the decisive turnings in the way of life called for in the living present, and the consideration of the end of our existence, our destiny—all these come to focus in the spiritual conversation known as pastoral counseling.[50]

Protestant Distinctives for Pastoral Counseling

Within the Protestant or Free Church tradition, Wayne Oates has selected four "salient" principles that direct the "meaning, purpose, and function" of the Protestant counselor.[51] The first is *the sovereign Lordship of Christ.* Protestant pastoral counseling begins with an affirmation of faith in God. It is therefore faced against human endeavors to deify anything within the created order. So many painful episodes in life that bring people to pastoral counselors relate to the loss of or threatened loss of their idols. The goal of Protestant pastoral counselors is to challenge all forms of idolatry, but also to comfort people in their bereavement over lost idols. A primary methodology for pastoral counselors is to introduce or reintroduce the counselee to the worship of God in Christ as a "center" around which a new and more satisfying life can be built.

The second principle is *the dialogue between Creator and creature.* Oates calls attention to the truth that God is available for personal dialogue through which the sufferers may draw strength to clarify and decide on the way(s) in which to respond to their problems.

Third, the principle of *the consecration of life and the priesthood of all believers* insists that no part of existence is "common or unclean," nor is any one person more "consecrated" than any other. The Christian community is one of mutual burden bearing. It is the duty of all Christians to "serve one another in love." Although pastors and pastoral counseling specialists continue to proliferate, the tasks of pastoral counseling belong to every member of the Christian community. Pastoral counseling must be seen as the duty of the fellowship of believers making "the private practice of pastoral counseling apart from the life of the church . . . a violation of the basic character of the ministry, if not an active violation of professional ethics."[52]

The final principle is that of *the release from the bondage of self-justification into the freedom of justification by faith,* rooted in the results of the work of Christ, activated by the confrontational confession-forgiveness-acceptance process of a counseling session, and confirmed in the prayerful relationship of the counselee with God. The work of grace occurs, self-condemnation is overcome, and the counselee is free to live in newness of life.

Contributions from the Free Church Tradition

Two additional emphases from the Protestant Reformation deserve reflection by pastors and pastoral counseling specialists. First, Reformation theologians made much of Jesus' admonition to his disciples to "call no man . . . father" (Matt. 23:9). Jesus related to and called his disciples his friends (John 15:14), and Abraham was known as a friend of God (James 2:23). The persistence of over-under relationships in which the pastor or counselor is dominant and the parishioner or counselee is submissive is all too evident in contemporary Protestant ministry patterns and institutional practice. These patterns perpetuate a pre-Reformation episcopal style of clerical functioning and ignore the historic Protestant rediscovery of the healing power of relational equality.

The second additional Protestant Reformation distinctive is the power of persons in face-to-face relationships guided by a spiritual covenant to deal with the damage inflicted on persons by sin. Furthermore, this same face-to-face community can provide effective nurture and healing in the aftermath of the experience of forgiveness of sin. This New Testament rediscovery on the part of the Radical Reformers was in large measure a protest against the assumed sacramental monopoly of the Roman Catholic Church and its claims of exclusive possession of spiritual healing. A restudy of this Reformation distinctive and a revision of pastoral care and counseling procedures based on such a study would greatly enrich contemporary Protestant pastoral practice. A careful rereading of the Oates writings will reveal his attempt to deal consistently and faithfully with these two theological emphases of the Protestant Reformers in his own teaching and practice of pastoral care and counseling.

The Pastor's Counseling Methodologies

The practical application of theological principles for pastoral counseling is also an important part of the Oates agenda for pastoral counseling. In brief outline form, the goals and process of the pastoral exploratory, or short-term counseling interview, is as follows.[53] First, a covenant of time is established, such as, "Let's invest the next thirty minutes in talking about this matter." Second, the issue is explored in a "hearing out" manner. Third, a detailed inquiry directed by the pastor is conducted. Fourth, all possible alternatives are explored, including the spiritual meanings of the issues at stake and the relationship these may have to the ongoing purposes of God. Fifth, the pastor offers appropriate spiritual support and guidance as the painbearer makes a decision. Sixth, a final interpretation is made, additional support is given, and a covenant of continuing concern is offered by the pastor.

Longer-term "progressively more profound and complex meetings or interviews" are also the standard practice of the pastor or pastoral counselor. Whatever the verbal exchanges between pastor and counselee, the initial agenda involves establishing a relationship of trust called by Oates *the removal of threat.* This includes a defusing of counselee anxiety revolving around the threats of being dominated, judging life to be meaningless, fearing exposure, fear of being used irresponsibly and of being irresponsible, and overcoming all reasons to be dishonest or phony within the counseling relationship.

The second phase is called *participant understanding.* The counselor and the counselee deal directly with the matters troubling the counselee which involve an understanding or new understanding of the past and the present, facing the conflicts arising between counselee values and actions, facing the bipolar struggle between the temptation to sin and the possibility to choose an ethical life, and a phase of self-encounter where the counselee is supported sufficiently to accept responsibility for self.

The third phase, *covenant making,* is the pastoral heart of the counseling process. In the covenant of confrontation, the counselee chooses to face reality, however painful, and moves to the covenant of confession to the counselor and to God. Then the counselee experiences the covenant of forgiveness and restitution, first as recipient and then as grace giver to others. Finally comes the covenant of concern, in which the counselee experiences a commitment to change because of the deep concerns which have been focused and resolved.

The counseling then moves to the phase of *community involvement,* in which the counselee moves out into the patterns of everyday life of love, work, and worship as a way to "test and affirm" the decisions earnestly made in the counseling process.[54]

A final methodology of note is Oates's use of prayer in pastoral counseling. Because prayer is another name for relationship to God, prayer is not a means to an end; it can be an important aspect of the counseling process. "Pastoral counseling, when properly understood, is in and of itself a total experience of prayer."[55]

The reporting of, or experiencing of, a counselee's prayers will reveal feelings of hope or despair and indicate the person's sense of doom or destiny. The prayer life of a person v. ill reflect the quality of that person's relationship to God, aspects of anger, feelings of disappointment or disillusionment, and feelings of having been abandoned by God. Of crucial importance in pastoral counseling is to discover whether the counselee expects ready-made answers from God or whether God's presence and support are sought for a more independent solution to the present difficulty.[56] Information about a person's use of religion, involvement in fantasy or reality, as well as the quality and depth of a counselee's faith, are all available when the counselor is privy to the life of prayer.[57]

A counselee's capacity and willingness to relate to God are important indicators of spiritual strength and capacity for intimacy. Teaching a counselee to grow in prayer is a way to strengthen all the systems for health and hope. It also opens the way for the Holy Spirit to work in the session and help "both the counselor and the counselee to understand in his own language the truth that God would have them both to know."[58]

Other Major Contributions

No introduction to the Oates agenda for pastoral care would be complete without specific mention of his substantial contributions to the literature of religion and mental health.[59] In his own focused writing in the specialty field of psychiatry and religion, two major principles lead all the rest. The first proclaims idolatry as the major religious factor in mental illness. Set in a framework of the value of religion as a diagnostic tool to detect mental ill health, Oates demonstrates the clinical value of religious dialogue with mentally disturbed persons. Their practices of giving ultimate loyalties to finite objects are the "seed bed" of their illnesses.

The second principle affirms the restorative and rehabilitative value of the biblical practice of the face-to-face covenant community of caring believers. Such a community can provide an efficient cure of mentally disturbed persons today by the careful following of directions given in the Christian Scriptures.

Other important areas of the Oates agenda deserve mention in this brief overview. Among these are the pastoral task of preaching (including published sermons as well as instructional comments about preaching),[60] specific attention to pastoral care interventions related to social problems,[61] instructions and written encouragement for laypersons in a variety of the more uncomfortable situations in life,[62] specific comments regarding theological education and the preparation of pastoral ministers,[63] and specific comments related to the academic and practical aspects of the psychology of religion.[64]

Evaluative Comments

This brief discussion has presented selected items from the Oates agenda for pastoral care without extensive evaluation. In conclusion, a few words of critical comment are in order.

First, Wayne Oates has been criticized for being "provincial." His use of thought patterns and illustrations, his critics maintain, is decidedly rural and reflects the culture of the Southeastern states. Religiously, his theological constructs are Baptist with a decidedly "Southern" flavor. His choice of face-to-face, two-way covenant methods of relationship and vigorous rejection of hierarchical relational methods guided by closed standards and procedures are frequently seen as irregular. One of the consequences of these preferences has been an ongoing debate with pastoral care persons of other denominations in the arena of national bodies for the certification of clinical pastoral educators and pastoral counselors.

His response to his critics, both publicly and privately, is to call attention to the fact that everyone speaks from some cultural bias. He simply "owns" his own. In print and in person, he is all these things and more. But it is also true that he has lectured, published, and consulted in a wide ecumenical arena. His experience supports Harry Stack Sullivan's comment that people are all more human than otherwise. I sense that what he has seen through his provincial eyes is more universally applicable than subregionally bound. The criticism that he is provincial stands, but my judgment is that his own uniquely polarized writing both clarifies his positions and enables others to clarify their own in relationship to him.

A second criticism relates to his being labeled by some as a fundamentalist, or certainly a biblicist. So many of his presuppositions, theoretical constructs, and practical procedures are expressed in biblical quotations. It is a rare subsection in his writing which does not include a Bible verse or a biblical paraphrase. With this criticism, Oates disagrees agreeably! Even a casual glance at his utilization of Scripture relieves him of the fundamentalist charge. He is not an inerrantist. Fundamentalists are! He accepts and makes use of higher critical methods of biblical studies and uses historical, textual, linguistic, and form-critical methods routinely. Freed by these disciplines, he is not enslaved to the literal text of the Bible and therefore does not deserve the "biblicist" label.

That he is a man of the Bible, that he proclaims the ability of the Scriptures to effect a supernatural dialogue between human beings and God, and that the distilled wisdom of a loving God of creation is stored in the pages of the Judeo-Christian Scriptures, he affirms in all he writes, teaches, and preaches. But he is neither fundamentalist nor biblicist.

A third criticism relates to Oates's style. He has been accused of cluttering his writings with so many quotations and paraphrases that his own points are masked, a criticism less likely to be leveled during the last ten years of his productive period. He is especially accused of writing about supernatural subjects with even less precision. Oates simply accepts this criticism with an invitation to his critics to write about these subjects themselves. He has written with the clarity available from his current angle of vision.

A final criticism of his style deserves special comment. He has been accused of writing in a standard sermonic style. To this Oates replies, "All too true." By vocation, he is primarily a pastor, and one of his major responsibilities is proclamation. To that responsibility he has been faithful. He intends his writings to be persuasive. He intends that his readers, largely pastors also, adapt his materials into their own literary and sermonic activities. He has published sermons in many places and has an entire book of sermons in print. And he hopes all who read his materials will be stimulated to begin or to intensify a personal relationship with the God who has revealed himself in Jesus Christ.

Notes

1. Finding Center in Pastoral Care / *Thornton*

1. "Two Tales by Martin Buber," in Jean Sulzberger, *Search* (Harper & Row, 1979), p. 3.

2. John C. Wynn's *Family Therapy in Pastoral Ministry* (Harper & Row, 1982) marks our progress toward systems pastoral care of the family. James E. Dittes, *The Church in the Way* (Charles Scribner's Sons, 1967), posed an early challenge to pastoral care to integrate individual and system perspectives in the pastoral functions of leadership and administration. Others pressed the point upon chaplains and therapists in relation to their roles in institutional and agency systems. (See G. Douglass Lewis, ed., *Explorations in Ministry: A Report on the Ministry in the 70's Project,* An IDOC Dossier. 637 West 125th Street, New York, N.Y., 1971.)

3. Dittes, *The Church.*

4. A conversation with Frederick Kuether, 1959.

5. Abraham H. Maslow, *Toward a Psychology of Being* (D. Van Nostrand Co., 1968), pp. 71–125.

6. Daniel N. Leininger, "The Psychology of Abraham H. Maslow and A Pastoral Theology of Grace" (Ph.D. dissertation, Southern Baptist Theological Seminary, 1979), pp. 99–101.

7. Abraham H. Maslow, *Religions, Values and Peak-Experiences* (Viking Press, 1964), p. 66.

8. Ibid., pp. 288–291.

9. Abraham H. Maslow, *The Farther Reaches of Human Nature* (Viking Press, 1971), p. 279.

10. The marks of this state of consciousness are well-documented in the literature beginning with William James, *The Varieties of Religious Experience* (Modern Library, 1902), and coming to a high point of documentation and clarity in Ken Wilber, *The Atman Project: A Transpersonal View of Human Development* (Theosophical Publishing House, 1980), and *A Sociable God: A Brief Introduction to a Transcendental Sociology* (McGraw-Hill Book Co., 1982).

11. Maslow, *Farther Reaches.*

12. For a depth analysis of will and willingness in the spiritual life, see Gerald G. May, M.D., *Will and Spirit: A Contemplative Psychology* (Harper & Row, 1982).

13. Thomas Merton, *The New Man* (Farrar, Straus & Cudahy, 1961), pp. 23–50.

14. See also James E. Loder, *The Transforming Moment: Understanding Convictional Experiences* (Harper & Row, 1981), for a discussion of negation as the fourth pole of transforming development.

15. Martin E. Marty, *A Cry of Absence: Reflections for the Winter of the Heart* (Harper & Row, 1983).

16. See also Wolfhart Pannenberg, *Christian Spirituality* (Westminster Press, 1983), pp. 71–92; and Merton, *New Man,* pp. 23–50.

17. Leon Morris, in a study of love in the Bible, finds to his amazement that the literature of both Old and New Testament theology ignores love altogether as a major theme or relates it to a minor place. Selective inattention such as this among biblical theologians may be symptomatic of the prevalence of "Promethean theology," as Merton describes it. See Leon Morris, *Testaments of Love: A Study of Love in the Bible* (Wm. B. Eerdmans Publishing Co., 1981).

18. Wayne E. Oates, *Nurturing Silence in a Noisy Heart* (Doubleday & Co., 1979).

19. Some guides you can trust are the following: Morton T. Kelsey, *The Other Side of Silence: A Guide to Christian Meditation* (Paulist Press, 1976); John Killinger, *Prayer: The Act of Being with God* (Word Books, 1981); Lawrence LeShan, *How to Meditate: A Guide to Self-discovery* (Bantam Books, 1975); Gerald G. May, *The Open Way: A Meditation Handbook* (Paulist Press, 1977); Edward E. Thornton, *Being Transformed: An Inner Way of Spiritual Growth* (Westminster Press, 1984); Ronald V. Wells, *Spiritual Disciplines for Everyday Living* (Character Research Press, 1982).

20. Gerald G. May, M.D., *Care of Mind—Care of Spirit: Psychiatric Dimensions of Spiritual Direction* (Harper & Row, 1982).

21. James W. Fowler, *Stages of Faith: The Psychology of Human Development and the Quest for Meaning* (Harper & Row, 1981).

22. Ana-Maria Rizzuto, *The Birth of the Living God: A Psychoanalytic Study* (University of Chicago Press, 1979).

23. Loder, *Transforming Moment.*

24. Task Force on Nomenclature and Statistics of the American Psychiatric Association, *Diagnostic and Statistical Manual of Mental Disorders,* 3rd ed. (American Psychiatric Association, 1980).

25. M. Scott Peck, *People of the Lie: The Hope for Healing Human Evil* (Simon & Schuster, 1983).

26. Wilber, *A Sociable God,* pp. 59–61.

27. See a comprehensive survey and classification by C. Roy Woodruff, *Alcoholism and Christian Experience* (Westminster Press, 1968).

2. Recovering the Pastor's Role as Spiritual Guide / *Hinson*

1. Clement of Alexandria, *Stromateis* 1.1.18.1–4.

2. Ibid., 2.21–22.

3. Ibid., 4.23.

4. Ibid., 5.12.

5. Ibid., 7.12.77; Henry Chadwick and J. E. L. Oulton, eds., *Alexandrian Christianity,* Library of Christian Classics, Vol. 2 (Westminster Press, 1977), p. 142.

6. Bernard of Clairvaux, *The Letters of St. Bernard of Clairvaux,* tr. by Bruno Scott James (London: Burns, Oates & Washbourne, 1953), p. 43.

7. Margaret Cropper, *Life of Evelyn Underhill* (Harper & Brothers, 1958), p. 75.

8. Kenneth Leech, *Soul Friend: A Study of Spirituality* (London: Sheldon Press, 1977), pp. 88–89.

9. Douglas V. Steere, *On Listening to Another,* in Doubleday Devotional Classics, ed. by E. Glenn Hinson (Doubleday & Co., 1978), pp. 205–257.

4. The Power of Spiritual Language in Self-understanding / *Oates*

1. Charles V. Gerkin, *The Living Human Document: Re-Visioning Pastoral Counseling in a Hermeneutical Mode* (Abingdon Press, 1984), p. 26.

2. Daniel J. Boorstin, *The Discoverers* (Random House, 1983), pp. 521–523.

3. John Calvin, *The Institutes of the Christian Religion,* tr. by Henry Beveridge (Wm. B. Eerdmans Publishing Co., 1953), I.iii.4, pp. 544–545.

4. Dietrich Bonhoeffer, *Creation and Fall: A Theological Interpretation of Genesis 1–3* (Macmillan Co., 1959), p. 98.

5. Friedrich Nietzsche, *Thus Spoke Zarathustra,* tr. by R. J. Hollingdale (Penguin Books, 1961), p. 67.

6. Bonhoeffer, *Creation,* p. 98.

7. Carl Jung, *Modern Man in Search of a Soul* (Harcourt, Brace and Co., 1955), p. 91.

8. Alan Paton, *Cry, the Beloved Country* (Charles Scribner's Sons, 1948), pp. 229, 230, 232.

5. The New Language of Pastoral Counseling / *Patton*

1. Task Force on Nomenclature and Statistics of the American Psychiatric Association, *Diagnostic and Statistical Manual of Mental Disorders,* 3rd ed. (American Psychiatric Association, 1980).

2. Heinz Kohut, *The Restoration of the Self* (International Universities Press, 1977), pp. 67–68.

3. Roy Schafer, *Language and Insight: The Sigmund Freud Lectures at University College, London* (Yale University Press, 1978), p. 7.

4. Roy Schafer, *A New Language for Psychoanalysis* (Yale University Press, 1976), pp. 128–129.

5. John Patton, "An Anniversary Pastime," *The Journal of Pastoral Care,* Vol. 29, No. 1 (March 1975), p. 1.

6. Carl R. Rogers, as quoted by John M. Schlien, "Phenomenology and Personality," in *Concepts of Personality,* ed. by Joseph M. Wepman and Ralph W. Heine (Aldine Publishing Co., 1963), p. 315.

7. Carl R. Rogers, "Persons or Science? A Philosophical Question," in *On Becoming a Person* (Houghton Mifflin Co., 1970), p. 218.

8. Charles V. Gerkin, *The Living Human Document: Re-Visioning Pastoral Counseling in a Hermeneutical Mode* (Abingdon Press, 1984).

9. Karl Menninger, *Theory of Psychoanalytic Technique* (Basic Books, 1958), p. 129.

10. Susan Handelman, "Interpretation as Devotion," *The Psychoanalytic Review,* Vol. 68, No. 2 (Summer 1981), pp. 201–217.

11. Walker Percy, *The Moviegoer* (Avon Books, 1979), p. 18.

12. John Patton, "The Secret of Pastoral Counseling," *The Journal of Pastoral Care,* Vol. 26, No. 2 (June 1972).

13. Paul W. Pruyser, *The Minister as Diagnostician: Personal Problems in Pastoral Perspective* (Westminster Press, 1976), ch. 5.

14. Seward Hiltner, "Implications for the Ministry of the Dialogue Between Doctrine and Experience," *Report of the Sixth Biennial Meeting of the Association of Seminary Professors in the Practical Fields,* Richmond, Va., June 10–13, 1960, p. 74.

15. See, e.g., Ray L. Hart, *Unfinished Man and the Imagination: Toward an Anthology and a Rhetoric of Revelation* (Seabury Press, 1979), and Theodore W. Jennings, Jr., *Introduction to Theology: An Invitation to Reflection Upon the Christian Myths* (Fortress Press, 1976).

16. John Patton, "Your Present and Silence," *The Journal of Pastoral Care,* Vol. 26, No. 2 (June 1972), p. 73.

17. John Patton, *Pastoral Counseling: A Ministry of the Church* (Abingdon Press, 1983), chs. 1 to 3.

6. Pastoral Care with the Aged:
The Spiritual Dimension / *Meiburg*

1. Paul B. Maves and J. Lennart Cedarleaf, *Older People and the Church* (Abingdon-Cokesbury Press, 1949).

2. Nathan W. Shock, "Medical/Biological Research on Aging: A Comment," *Aging: Research and Perspectives,* Columbia Journalism Monograph No. 3 (Graduate School of Journalism, Columbia University, 1979), p. 26. Subsequent references to this document are abbreviated as Columbia Journalism Monograph No. 3.

3. Ibid., p. 27.

4. Ibid.

5. Robert N. Butler, "Breaking Images: The Media and Aging," Columbia Journalism Monograph No. 3, p. 2.

6. Elaine M. Brody, "Social, Economic, and Environmental Issues Relating to Aging," Columbia Journalism Monograph No. 3, p. 39.

7. Cited by Brody, "Social, Economic, and Environmental Issues," p. 40.

8. Ibid., p. 41.

9. In Bernice L. Neugarten, ed., *Middle Age and Aging: A Reader in Social Psychology* (University of Chicago Press, 1968).

10. Sarah-Patton Boyle, *The Desert Blooms: A Personal Adventure in Growing Old Creatively* (Abingdon Press, 1983).

11. William Clements, in *The Journal of Religion and Health,* Vol. 18, No. 2 (1979).

12. Boyle, *The Desert Blooms,* p. 143.

13. The address is reprinted in Carol LeFevre and Perry LeFevre, eds., *Aging and the Human Spirit: A Reader in Religion and Gerontology* (Exploration Press, Chicago Theological Seminary, 1981), pp. 35–44.

7. Revisioning the Future of Spirit-centered Pastoral Care and Counseling / *Clinebell*

1. John Naisbitt, *Megatrends: Ten New Directions Transforming Our Lives* (Warner Communications, 1982), p. 84.

2. Alvin Toffler, *The Third Wave* (Bantam Books, 1981); Daniel Yankelovich, *New Rules: Searching for Self-fulfillment in a World Turned Upside Down* (Random House, 1981); and Naisbitt, *Megatrends.*

3. Toffler, *The Third Wave,* p. 14.

4. Gerald Gurin, Joseph Veroff, and Sheila Feld, *Americans View Their Mental Health* (Basic Books, 1960).

5. Joseph Veroff, Richard A. Kulka, and Elizabeth Dorran, *Mental Health in America* (Basic Books, 1981).

6. Naisbitt, *Megatrends,* p. 282.

7. Ibid., ch. 2.

8. Yankelovich, *New Rules.*

9. Carol Gilligan, *In a Different Voice: Psychological Theory and Women's Development* (Harvard University Press, 1982).

10. Jean Baker Miller, *Toward a New Psychology of Women* (Beacon Press, 1977).

11. Howard Clinebell, *Basic Types of Pastoral Care and Counseling* (Abingdon Press, 1984).

12. Robert McAfee Brown, *Making Peace in the Global Village* (Westminster Press, 1981); J. Christopher Grannis et al., *The Risk of the Cross: Christian Discipleship in the Nuclear Age* (Seabury Press, 1981); Ronald J. Sider and Richard K. Taylor, *Nuclear Holocaust and Christian Hope: A Book for Christian Peacemakers* (Inter-Varsity Press, 1982); and David P. Barash and Judith E. Lipton, *Stop Nuclear War! A Handbook* (Grove Press, 1982).

13. Joanna R. Macy, *Despair and Personal Power in the Nuclear Age* (New Society Publishers, 1983).

14. Norman Cousins, *Anatomy of an Illness as Perceived by the Patient: Reflections on Healing and Regeneration* (W. W. Norton & Co., 1979).

8: The Oates Agenda for Pastoral Care / *Jackson*

1. Wayne E. Oates, *The Struggle to Be Free: My Story and Your Story* (Westminster Press, 1983). The biographical comments in this section follow this autobiographical book.

2. Ibid., p. 23.

3. Wayne E. Oates, *The Bible in Pastoral Care* (Westminster Press, 1953), pp. 15–27.

4. Wayne E. Oates, *Christ and Selfhood* (Association Press, 1961), pp. 234–237, and *Protestant Pastoral Counseling* (Westminster Press, 1962), pp. 57–58.

5. Oates, *Christ and Selfhood,* p. 235.

6. Ibid., p. 237.

7. Wayne E. Oates, *Religious Dimensions of Personality* (Association Press, 1957), pp. 270–273.

8. *Christ and Selfhood,* pp. 35–37.

9. *Religious Dimensions of Personality,* pp. 297–304.

10. Ibid., pp. 292–297.

11. *Christ and Selfhood,* pp. 21–23.

12. Ibid., p. 75.

13. Ibid., pp. 74–101.

14. *Religious Dimensions of Personality,* pp. 24–25.

15. Wayne E. Oates, *The Significance of the Work of Sigmund Freud for the Christian Faith* (Th.D. dissertation, Southern Baptist Theological Seminary, 1947), p. ii.

16. Ibid.

17. Wayne E. Oates, *Pastoral Counseling* (Westminster Press, 1981), pp. 198–199; *Christ and Selfhood,* p. 94.

18. Wayne E. Oates, *The Christian Pastor,* 3rd ed. (Westminster Press, 1982), pp. 34–35.

19. *Religious Dimensions of Personality,* pp. 43–44.

20. Wayne E. Oates, *The Christian Pastor,* 1st ed. (Westminster Press, 1951).

21. *The Christian Pastor,* 3rd ed., p. 9.

22. Wayne E. Oates, *New Dimensions of Pastoral Care* (Fortress Press, 1970), p. 3.

23. *The Christian Pastor,* 3rd ed., pp. 29–63.

24. Wayne E. Oates, *Anxiety in Christian Experience* (Westminster Press, 1955), pp. 15–46, 77–99.

25. Ibid., pp. 51–55.

26. Wayne E. Oates, *Your Particular Grief* (Westminster Press, 1981), pp. 23–109.

27. Ibid., p. 96.

28. *New Dimensions of Pastoral Care,* pp. 29–30.

29. *The Christian Pastor,* 3rd ed., pp. 68, 69.

30. *Religious Dimensions of Personality,* pp. 222–226.

31. *The Christian Pastor,* 3rd ed., pp. 83–89.

32. Ibid., p. 89.

33. *The Christian Pastor*, 2nd ed., p. 68.

34. Ibid., p. 55. The emphasis is Oates's.

35. Ibid., p. 139.

36. *The Christian Pastor,* 3rd ed., pp. 262, 268.

37. Ibid., Chapters VI and VII.

38. *The Christian Pastor,* 2nd ed., p. 162.

39. Quoted in *The Christian Pastor,* 3rd ed., p. 211 (Oates's emphasis).

40. Ibid., p. 214.

41. Ibid., p. 216.

42. Ibid., pp. 220–222.

43. Ibid., p. 224.

44. Ibid., p. 283.

45. Wayne E. Oates, ed., *Introduction to Pastoral Counseling* (Broadman Press, 1959), p. iv.

46. *Protestant Pastoral Counseling* (see Note 4), p. 38.

47. *Religious Dimensions of Personality,* p. 253.

48. *Protestant Pastoral Counseling,* pp. 104, 107.

49. *Pastoral Counseling,* p. 14.

50. *Protestant Pastoral Counseling,* pp. 164–165.

51. Ibid., p. 24.

52. Ibid., pp. 29, 30, 31–32.

53. Wayne E. Oates, "The Temporary or Short Term Interview," *Introduction to Pastoral Counseling,* pp. 108–116.

54. *Protestant Pastoral Counseling,* pp. 172–188.

55. Wayne E. Oates, "Pastoral Counseling and the Experience of Prayer," *Introduction to Pastoral Counseling,* p. 211.

56. Ibid., p. 213.

57. Ibid., pp. 215–216.

58. Ibid., p. 211.

59. Wayne E. Oates, *When Religion Gets Sick* (1970), *Anxiety in Christian Experience* (1972), and *The Religious Care of the Psychiatric Patient* (1978), all from Westminster Press.

60. Wayne E. Oates, *The Revelation of God in Human Suffering* (Westminster Press, 1959).

61. Wayne E. Oates, *Alcohol: In and Out of the Church* (Broadman Press, 1966), and *Pastoral Counseling in Social Problems: Extremism, Race, Sex, Divorce* (Westminster Press, 1966).

62. Wayne E. Oates, *Life's Detours* (Upper Room, 1974), *Nurturing Silence in a Noisy Heart* (Doubleday & Co., 1979), and *Your Particular Grief* (Westminster Press, 1981).

63. Wayne E. Oates, *New Dimensions of Pastoral Care* (see Note 22) and "Organizational Development and Pastoral Care," *Review and Expositor*, Vol. 75 (1978), pp. 343–360.

64. Wayne E. Oates, *Religious Dimensions of Personality* (see Note 7) and *The Psychology of Religion* (Word Books, 1973).